How to Present Like a Pro

Getting People to See Things Your Way

Lani Arredondo

Corporate Trainer and Speaker
Resource Associates

McGraw-Hill, Inc.

New York St. Louis San Francisco Auckland Bogotá
Caracas Hamburg Lisbon London Madrid Mexico
Milan Montreal New Delhi Paris
San Juan São Paulo Singapore
Sydney Tokyo Toronto

Library of Congress Cataloging-in-Publication Data

Arredondo, Lani.
  How to present like a pro / Lani Arredondo.
    p.   cm.
  ISBN 0-07-002506-1—ISBN 0-07-002505-3 (pbk.)
  1. Business presentations. 2. Oral communication. 3. Public
speaking. I. Title.
HF5718.22.A77 1991
658.4'52—dc20   90-31478
                                    CIP

      6 7 8 9 0 DOC/DOC 9 6 5 4 3

ISBN 0-07-002506-1
ISBN 0-07-002505-3 {PBK.}

*The sponsoring editor for this book was James H. Bessent, Jr., the editing
supervisor was Marion B. Castellucci, the designer was Naomi Auerbach, and
the production supervisor was Suzanne W. Babeuf. This book was set in
Baskerville. It was composed by McGraw-Hill's Professional & Reference
Division composition unit.*

Printed and bound by R. R. Donnelley & Sons Company.

This book is printed on recycled, acid-free paper containing a minimum of 50% recycled de-
inked fiber.

To Jess
For the time and loving encouragement

About the Author

Lani Arredondo is the founder and principal of Resource
Associates, a California-based consulting and training firm.
Formerly a manager and marketeer at IBM — where she
earned several awards — Ms. Arredondo is a veteran
presenter with more than 20 years' experience in making
presentations in corporate, classroom, and guest-speaker
settings. She has trained and coached managers and staff at
Eastman Kodak, IBM, Pacific Bell, and other major
organizations. An honors graduate of the University of
California, Ms. Arredondo is on the faculty of the National
University's School of Business and Management.

Contents

Preface

Who wrote *In Search of Excellence*? Most business people would readily answer, "Tom Peters." Who was the coauthor of the book? That question draws blank stares from a lot of people. Others furrow their brows in thought. In more than one group I've addressed, someone in the audience would answer, "That other guy."

Who's headed Chrysler Corporation? Without hesitation, most people answer, "Lee Iacocca." And who heads General Motors? "Uhm . . ."

What distinguishes some people from their counterparts or competitors and makes them more memorable? Why are names like Peters and Iacocca synonymous with success while others go relatively unnoticed? What is it they do that the "other guys" don't? In a word, they *present!*

We notice dynamic presenters because they're noticeably center stage. They're not there because they're better looking or more intelligent. After all, you can always find others who are equally or better qualified in those respects. Nor are they there because they have superior social or political ties. While that may help, a person who displays skill can gain the advantage.

People occupy center stage when they have something meaningful to say and the ability to say it very well. They present themselves and their messages with confidence and conviction. They have mastered the art of presenting in a way that captures people's hearts and minds.

If you want to captivate people, remember the familiar adage, "Out of sight, out of mind." When you present skillfully, you're very much "in sight and in mind." We see the principle at work all the time in sports, entertainment, and politics. It's at work in every other arena as well: in business, government, education, and religion. In almost every field of endeavor, the ability to present can pay high dividends.

In his popular book, *Bringing Out the Best in People*, Alan McGinnis points out, "You can gain a considerable following if you are willing to relate your message to enough people."[1] If you're interested in career visibility and advancement; if you're involved in community projects and you need to solicit support; if you're a manager who wants to influence employees and peers; or you're a salesperson who wants customers to buy—then you need to gain a following. When you want to attract attention to yourself or approval for the policies or proposals you present, then you want to gain a following.

The person with the greater following of advocates obviously has the competitive edge. Having followers implies you possess leadership skills (a hot issue in management circles today). Having a following indicates you have people's acceptance and approval, essential ingredients for success. Of the ways to gain a following, masterful presenting is one of the best.

Do you network? Great. So does just about everyone else. Do you have a mentor? Great. What's to say they'll always be around? Do you present? No? Then you may be missing out. Nothing else (short of outstanding performance) so distinguishes a person from the crowd as demonstrating the ability to stir that crowd. Presenting is a wonderful vehicle for doing that, an opportunity for exposure.

But the secret isn't just in presenting. It's in presenting very well. There are, after all, two kinds of exposure: the kind you want and the kind you don't! Gaining a following and favorable exposure depends on delivering effective presentations.

What does it mean to be effective? The notable and quotable management consultant, Peter Drucker, defined it as "doing the right things." An effective presenter is one who "does the right things" and thus gains the most from every presentation.

What are the "right things" to do when you present? They're described in the chapters that follow. The first lays a foundation of five basic principles that are critical to a presenter's success. In chapters two through four, you'll become acquainted with techniques that enable you to present like a PRO (Prepare, Relate, Optimize). You'll discover how to prepare material easily; how to relate it to people meaningfully (whether you're addressing an audience of one or one thousand); and how to optimize your effectiveness through style and delivery. Additional chapters provide insights into the selection and use of audiovisual media;

---

[1]Alan Loy McGinnis, *Bringing Out the Best in People*, Augsburg Publishing House, Minneapolis, 1985, p. 167.

how to handle difficult situations; and how to build your confidence before a group.

When you know how to deliver effective "right things" presentations, you'll project your knowledge and ideas in a way that captures people's attention and secures their approval. You'll enjoy the gratification that comes from having a potentially powerful impact on people. And, you'll be remembered. Not just as the "other guy" or gal, but as a capable and confident professional.

That's what this book is about. It's not about public speaking. I'm not interested in encouraging the propagation of any more public speakers. There are already quite enough of them around. I am, however, very interested in encouraging the development of skillful presenters. There aren't nearly enough of them around. The differences between the two are subtle, but perceptible.

It's a difference, first, of approach. The subject of public speaking is typically approached from the standpoint of the speaker. You know it's public speaking when you hear lingo like *elocution, oratory,* and *enunciation.* Such an academic approach emphasizes the role of the speaker, often to the detriment of the public. Frequently, the result is a meaningless speech that bogs down in a mire of dull data.

The subject of presenting, on the other hand, is approached from the standpoint of the audience. It takes, to coin a term from marketing jargon, a "consumer-focused" approach. It emphasizes who's listening. Presenting recognizes the public as the foremost element in any speaking situation, whether your public consists of employees, senior managers, customers, constituents, or a congregation.

The very definition of the word *present* is "to bring . . . to make a gift to." That implies a giver (a presenter) who's tuned in to what the recipient (the audience) wants. What response do you get when you give someone a gift of something they really want? That's the response you'll get when you present like a pro.

That's the second significant difference between public speaking and presenting—one of response. Poll a group of people and ask, "Which would you rather do: take a course in public speaking or do time in Siberia?" I'd venture to say more than a few will voice a preference for Siberia. Then ask, "Which would you rather do: listen to a public speaker or do time in Siberia?" A few more are likely to join the ranks for Siberia.

Why is that? It's because public speaking isn't perceived to be fun. Whether we're doing it or hearing it, all too often the experience isn't enlightening, entertaining, or satisfying. Audiences dread having to listen to yet one more dreary speech. You may dread being called on to make one. Presenting, on the other hand, is fun! It's exciting to know how to have an impact on people, to have your ideas and information well received. It's gratifying to see an audience moved by the message you're delivering to them. Understanding how to "package" the gift of your presentation so that it appeals to your listeners makes presenting enjoyable—for you and for them.

I recently taught presentation skills to a group of career people taking night courses to complete their college degrees. The group included, among others, a manager with a Fortune 500 company, a sales representative, a counselor for a substance-abuse program, a teacher, and a government agency administrator. They filed into the first class with expressions that ranged from boredom to obvious distaste. The prospect of public speaking didn't appeal to them.

At the outset of the course, everyone agreed that they'd seen very, very few good public speakers. By the end of the course, everyone agreed that they'd developed into very good presenters. They appeared more confident. They sounded more convincing. And they felt better equipped to do their jobs and to advance in them. They'd developed one more avenue for gaining a following, another set of skills that would contribute to their success.

Some suggested at the end of the course, "You ought to write a book." Others didn't need to say a word. Just observing how dramatically their presentations had improved was sufficient motivation for me. I've tried to capture here, in written form, what I present to clients and students "live."

I've seen people achieve success on the basis of good presentations and others lose out because of poor ones. I've listened to some presenters who inspired me to action and others who bored me to tears. I'd rather see people win. I'd rather be inspired than bored.

I'd like to be sitting in an audience one day hearing a presentation from someone who's read this book and applied its contents. If I've packaged this "presentation" properly, what I'll hear will be inspiring and what I'll see is a sure winner. I hope I have. And I hope it's you.

Lani Arredondo

1
Principles for Presenters

Every presentation you make (or have the chance to make) represents an opportunity to influence people. You can influence the way they think, how they perform their jobs, and with whom they do business. Through skillful presentation, you can impress upon people attitudes and ideas, new skills and techniques, the value of your products and services. You can demonstrate both your ability to communicate and your appeal as an individual.

After years in business and management, on sales calls and in classrooms, and on both sides of podiums, I've seen how the ability to present is crucial to achieving advancement for yourself and for your ideas. Few people make it to the top without first making it to their feet. Few people influence others—managers, subordinates, or customers—without understanding how to influence an audience.

As anyone who's sat in an audience knows, the ability to present is more than just the ability to speak or read out loud. You've probably been on the receiving end of presentations at least a few times yourself. It can be a numbing experience. If some speakers could see how badly they bore their listeners, they'd give serious consideration to what they could do to present more effectively.

When you're in the audience, do you feel captive, confined to your chair with no chance of escape? Are you nodding off as the minutes tick by like hours? Or do you feel captivated, fully engrossed in a dynamic presentation? Are you listening and alert as the minutes fly by unnoticed?

When you're the speaker, what happens when you step up to the podium, the head of the conference table, or the front of the room? Do you see attentive expressions on the faces staring back at you? Or glazed expressions, dulled by ennui? Are your "listeners" (maybe they're listening?) glued to their seats, hanging on to your every word? Or are they shifting restlessly, glancing at their watches, anxious to hear the last word?

What happens between presenter and audience depends in large part on the presenter's perspective. The best presenters take the view that presenting isn't formalized public speaking. It's a dynamic form of dealing with people. The best presenters address people (to borrow a colloquialism) "where they're at." Yet all too often we hear from speakers who appear unaware of what people need and want. They seem oblivious to what elicits a favorable audience response.

When you want to generate a favorable response, keep these principles in mind:

- The purpose of presenting is to persuade.
- Perceptions are more powerful than facts.
- People are inundated with data.
- People forget fast.
- Effective presentations are balanced and satisfy four basic criteria: they are attention-getting, meaningful, memorable, and activating.

We'll examine each of these principles further to establish their relationship to presenting. They're points you'll want to keep in mind as you prepare and deliver material to an audience.

The Purpose of Presenting Is to Persuade

Academic textbooks categorize speaking events as informative, social, public interest, or speeches to actuate. I assume *speeches to actuate* means, by definition, "presentations that move to action." In fact, each presentation should persuade people to act in response to your message. If it doesn't, there isn't much point in making the effort.

A great deal of human resources is present at every presentation. The speaker and the audience together represent a significant investment of time and money. Next time you attend a meeting or a conference, calculate the total amount of earnings represented by all those who are present. It may surprise you to realize how much is "lost" when a presentation is unproductive. People don't need to spend their time, as presenters or as listeners, without gaining something in return. The return is the action that occurs as a result of a persuasive presentation.

The action will vary, of course, depending on the nature of the event. From the audience's standpoint, it may mean they've gained information or insights that move them to behave in a different way. It may be that they're persuaded to sign a sales order. Or, it may mean they'll invite you back.

From your standpoint as a presenter, the resulting "action" can be tangible or intangible. It may take the form of personal gratification that comes from knowing the audience will make use of what you've presented. That you've successfully persuaded your listeners may result in an increase in your income, position, or status. Or it may mean they'll buy the books and cassettes you have on sale at the back of the room.

From one presentation to another, content, time frame, setting, norms, and audience composition vary. But all presentations have in common (regardless of textbook terms) the intent to persuade. It might be said that presenters are in the business of persuasion. We want people persuaded to listen and to learn, to accept us and our ideas, to act on our proposals or recommendations. Persuasion is the "bottom line."

Take the so-called informative presentation. A classic example would be a teacher or instructor presenting information to students in a classroom setting. Imagine if teachers presented from the perspective that their aim was to persuade. No more the droning lectures on English grammar and algebraic equations. Instead, we'd see lively, encouraging presentations that induced students to listen. We'd see teachers who persuasively conveyed the value of clarity and the power of numbers. Students would be more likely to respond affirmatively, and teachers would be more likely to satisfy their objectives.

Consider the social presentation. It's personified by the chairman of the board who makes a five-minute address at a sales convention or the guest speaker who talks for twenty minutes at a service club luncheon. The usual fare of cameo-appearance speakers serves to fill the agenda. Imagine hearing from a speaker who commanded your attention through persuasive presentation. It might just make it worth sitting through another chicken-plate special.

So-called public interest speeches are probably the worst examples of public speaking events. They're those "issues oriented" and "state of the state" messages that occur in governmental and sociopolitical settings, in hearings and public forums. We see them broadcast on television from the hallowed chambers of government buildings. We hear them from the spokespersons of special-interest groups. Typically, two kinds of speakers predominate in these settings.

There are the speakers who are sufficiently committed to the issue to suppress an internal fear of public speaking, but not sufficiently skilled to manage the external evidence of that fear. They clutch the podium, speaking down to its top. They read from a script in sleep-inducing monotones. They profess expertise but lack the confidence to present without relying on a script or teleprompter. As a consequence, they're not very persuasive. (I'm not poking fun at people who present like this. On the contrary, they have my deepest empathy. And they have my strongest encouragement. With proper training and coaching, even anxiety-ridden, podium-bound, script-dependent speakers can become invigorating, appealing presenters.)

At the other end of the spectrum of "public interest" speakers is what my mother would call "a poor substitute for Elmer Gantry." These speakers rely on podium-pounding passion to evoke support for an issue purportedly in the public interest. What they lack in substance, they attempt to make up for with an overabundance of style. They deliver the icing without the cake, the froth with too little filling. Dogmatic? Usually. Persuasive? To some. But the thoughtful listener is rarely convinced.

That brings us to the so-called speech to actuate. This is the truly persuasive presentation. The audience responds as the presenter intends, because the presenter attends to the audience. Persuasive presenters follow the "rules of the road"—the principles and techniques set forth in this book. They have in mind the overriding aim of serving their "customer," the audience. They recognize that speaking is intended for the benefit of their listeners. In turn, they reap benefits themselves from an audience that's been persuaded by what they've presented.

There's no better way to persuade people than to give them what they want. In the context of presenting, that amounts to delivering a message that really "speaks" to an audience, that gives them an experience they'll evaluate as having significant meaning. If every speaker approached presenting from the perspective of persuading, there would be many more effective and satisfied presenters and many more attentive and satisfied audiences.

Perception Is More Powerful Than Fact

A corollary to the principle of persuasion is that of perception. How an audience perceives a presenter can persuade them to, or dissuade them from, listening and responding. That's simply because what we perceive to be true carries more weight than what, in fact, is actually true.

In fact, you may be selling the best mousetrap on the market. But if people don't perceive that from the way you present it, they won't beat a path to your door. In fact, you may be a highly skilled technician with vital information to relate. But if people don't perceive that from the way you present, you'll lose your credibility and their attention.

It's a fact: Presenters who create positive perceptions generate opportunities and results. Presenters who are unaware of or unconcerned with how they're perceived risk having little influence on an audience or influencing them in a way they don't intend. To avoid that risk (especially in a presentation setting where you're the center of attention), you can ill afford to overlook anything that has an impact on the way you're perceived.

Perceptions are formed on three levels. Like computers, our minds (1) receive input and (2) process it. Unlike a computer, we then (3) make judgments in the context of our experience. While there's not much you can do about your listeners' previous experiences, there's a great deal you can do to shape the one they're having with you and what they'll perceive when you present. Effective presenters are aware of the power of perceptions and deliberately "design" themselves and their messages accordingly.

What an Audience Receives

A presentation isn't confined to just what you say or just what the audience hears. The audience responds on the basis of what they receive through all their senses. You present, and they receive through what you say verbally, how you sound vocally, and how it all looks visually. People are affected by the whole "package." They react, not just to the message, but to you and to the environment as well.

As if that weren't enough of a challenge, remember: People don't receive everything you present. They select what sparks their attention or what appeals to them. If you vocalize a thousand words, one person in the audience may subconsciously choose to take in five hundred. Another may select only three! What people in an audience select from your presentation depends on a number of factors.

Do they have sufficient interest in your topic, or more to the point, in how you're presenting it? Do they have a need for the information, or more to the point, are you creating a need? Are they harboring past experiences and conceptions (or misconceptions) that influence what they choose to receive? More to the point, are you creating for them a new and gratifying experience?

Assuming you create the interest, the need, and the positive experience that encourage people to receive most of your message, there is still the matter of how they process it.

What an Audience Processes

How do you enter data into a computer so that it processes information accurately? You follow an organized sequence of data input. Without a program that ensures conformance to standards of data entry and organization, you can make errors inputting the information. Input errors result in processing errors. Hence the phrase, "garbage in, garbage out." It applies to presentations as well.

Obviously, audiences aren't equipped with a "program" that eliminates input or processing errors. You communicate the words and phrases and paragraphs of your message onto a blank slate. (Actually, the minds receiving your message aren't literally blank, thanks to all the stuff that's affecting people's perceptions. But the illustration serves its purpose at this point.)

As the presenter, presumably you know what's on your mind. You know the points that are going to follow the point that you're making now. But the people you're addressing do not. To assimilate the bits and pieces of what they receive, they'll try to sort out and organize all the input. But they won't try very hard.

Most of us aren't trained to listen well. People won't put their minds to the task of organizing your message if the task is a strenuous one. If the input they receive is complicated, cluttered, or vague, the average audience will tune out. The overriding perception that will form in their minds is of a complicated, cluttered, or vague presenter.

I've seen it happen time and again. On one occasion, a highly qualified psychologist presented a workshop on interaction skills. He was a picture of the classic absent-minded professor. Reams of overhead transparencies were strewn about the table at which he worked. He hastily scrawled illegible notes on flip charts. He intended to use a cassette recording to support a point, but where, oh where, was the electrical outlet? The content of his message was excellent. It represented months invested in program development. But friends who attended the workshop with me remarked afterward, "He was so disorganized!" That's what they remembered of the presenter and the presentation.

Audiences won't do the organizing for you. You have to do it for them. It is, after all, your presentation. They'll perceive it in a more positive light if you make their job as listeners easy for them. That means preparing the content of your message in a well-organized manner (the subject of Chapter 2). It means eliminating distractions from the environment. It means using appropriate audiovisuals. It means doing all the right things to minimize "data entry and processing" errors. When you do, you increase the chances that they'll perceive what you've presented in the way you intended.

How an Audience Judges

The third factor in the perception process is a natural outcome of the first two. Having received and processed what's presented, people in the audience evaluate the experience. Generally, they don't do so as professionally trained critics on the basis of objective criteria. Instead, they form subjective opinions. They judge a presentation on the basis of how meaningful it was for them.

Have you ever attended a seminar and afterward talked with others who were also there? People's comments may have ranged from "That was great!" to "I didn't think it was so hot." That's a reflection of the power of perception and how subjective people's judgments are.

Assume you made a presentation last week. How did your listeners evaluate the experience you provided? The answer depends, in large part, on what you did to shape their perceptions. What did they see and hear? How orderly was the input and how easily were they able to process what they received? What meaning did they attach to your message? Was it the same meaning you intended to convey?

In many respects, presenting is an art. The whole room is your canvas. The facts are the fibers of your paintbrush. And brushstrokes alone do not a masterpiece make. It's how the brushstrokes are applied. Through the artful combination of all the elements of presenting, you create a "product" people perceive to be of value.

Some years ago, I attended a community business conference attended by a predominantly conservative male audience. The keynote speaker for the midday luncheon flew in from out of town and arrived unfashionably late. Word of her arrival must have been radioed ahead, because even as she was being introduced, she came dashing through the doors of the banquet hall. She rushed in, the epitome of a femme fatale. She was dressed in a miniskirt, low-cut blouse, and dangling earrings, and she sported a full mane of cascading hair. She hurriedly sprang up the steps to the speaker's platform and breathlessly took her place behind the podium. What a picture she painted!

Perception is more powerful than fact. And there aren't enough facts in a set of encyclopedias to recoup what that speaker lost during those first fateful sixty seconds! It wouldn't have mattered what information she presented. Every businesswoman in the audience cringed in embarrassment. Every businessman in the audience quickly formed an opinion. This was not a person to be taken seriously. People were talking about the incident weeks later. Unfortunately, what they remembered was not what this presenter had hoped they'd perceive.

Next time you prepare to present, ask yourself:

How do I want to be perceived to appeal to my viewers and listeners?

People Are Inundated With Data

In 1982, John Naisbitt brought the "information revolution" into focus with his best-selling book *Megatrends*. He observed that "we now mass-produce information the way we used to mass-produce cars."

He was followed the next year by Paul Hawken, author of *The Next Economy*. Commenting on what he termed the "informative economy," Hawken pointed out that we now live "in an information-rich environment where one is constantly challenged by new ideas" and that "there can be excess of information causing overload and stress."

There's currently such a proliferation of information that it's estimated the average American receives more than 2500 messages a day![1] It's not a surprising statistic when you consider the memos, letters, reports, publications, and files that stack up on your desk. Then there are those little telephone message slips that seem to reproduce as prolifically as rabbits!

Add to that the finding that white-collar professionals spend an average of 43 percent of their time in meetings and on the telephone.[2] In addition, various polls report that Americans spend an average of seven hours a day watching television—a medium rampant with messages. All things considered, 2500 messages a day seems a conservative estimate!

Findings like these ought to cause us to reflect. The people we address in presentations are victims—victims of what's been termed an "information explosion." In every audience are individuals who are swamped, inundated, overwhelmed by staggering volumes of information. What does that mean for you as a presenter? It means you're competing for people's attention. And the competition is fierce.

Even the most skilled presenters know: You never have everyone's full attention. The moment the momentum of a presentation drags, people's minds will wander. Mentally, they go off elsewhere. What's going on back at the office? What's going on back at home? What's going to go on at 5:15 when we can get out of here and head across the street for happy hour? (Hasn't that been true for you when you were in the audience?) All kinds of things occupy people's thoughts. That you have people's attendance does not guarantee that you have their attention.

As a guest speaker, you may have fifteen minutes in front of a group. As an instructor, you may have three hours. As a salesperson, you're fortunate to get an hour with a prospect. As a manager, you can chair a meeting as long as you wish, but the longer you do, the tougher keeping attention becomes.

Even when you have an opportunity to present, you don't have much of an opportunity. Consider this simple equation. Say you have two hours to present. You're addressing an audience that's awake sixteen hours a day, five working days a week. At the least, that's eighty hours a week that people in your audience receive messages, day in and day out. Your two hours with them represents little more than two percent of their time—this week. What other messages compete for their attention the other ninety-eight percent of the time?

The meaning in this message is clear. Presentations that just heap on information will be no more than grist for the mill. You have to do more than attempt to inform. If you want to have impact as a presenter, if you want to persuade people in an activating way, if your message is important to you and you want to make it important to them, you'd better be good!

That does not mean "naturally" good. While there may be a few "natural born" presenters out there, the majority of us have to learn how to present. We have to know how to prepare, package, and deliver the message we want people to accept. These are skills that can be learned.

The fear of speaking before groups is learned. Therefore, it can be unlearned. The habits we bring to platforms and podiums are learned. Therefore, new and improved habits can be learned as well. An "information dump" approach to presenting is learned (probably by attending too many public speaking events). It's an approach that can, and should, be unlearned.

I noted earlier that perceptions are more powerful than facts, and here I've presented facts. I've done so with the hope of creating a clearer perception of the problem of information overload. As presenters, we need to be aware that we're preparing and delivering a message for people who are already inundated with data.

One person who clearly understood this was my first training manager. Carol Wood hired and trained four of us novice presenters who came to be called "Carol's Girls." (Knowing Carol, that was a compliment.) It's been almost twenty years since I was under her tutelage, but I still remember her advice. It's especially appropriate in a society like ours that's so overloaded with information. It applies to everyone who's an "information bearer," which is anyone who presents.

> You don't need to tell people everything you know.
> Present only what they need to hear to be persuaded to accept your message.

People Forget Fast

A further challenge for those of us who present is that people forget fast. It's a consequence of information overload. Our brains are like an electrical circuit box. When the circuits are overloaded, they shut down. Or the storage capacity of a computer. When maximum capacity is reached, users erase data they perceive to be unnecessary or outdated.

Perhaps few presenters are more aware of this principle than instructors. We observe the results of short retention spans with every class. During a recent course I taught, which covered a span of four weeks, a third of the group forgot a key set of principles from the first week to the fourth. That was the result after I employed all the right things: interaction, repetition, visual aids, hands-on application, periodic progress checks, role playing...you name it. Imagine what the outcome would have been if I'd just lectured (heaven forbid!).

A marketing research study confirmed this point. A firm ran a newspaper ad once a week for thirteen weeks. Immediately afterwards, readers were surveyed. Sixty-three percent remembered the advertising. One month later, 32 percent recalled it. Two weeks after that, only 21 percent remembered it.[1] In a period of just six weeks, eight out of ten people had forgotten the printed message. If those statistics hold true for oral presentations, imagine: On the average, only two out of every ten people are going to remember a portion of what you say.

Does that make you feel like giving up on presenting? Ready to hang up your hat and leave the groups to someone else? Hold on to your hat! The news is not all bad. In fact, some of it's very good.

The good news is that effective presenters do make a difference. They've made a difference in my life. Chances are they've made a difference in yours. Dynamic presenters can have a very positive impact on individuals, on institutions, and on our culture. Consider the influence these presenters have had: Dale Carnegie, Norman Vincent Peale, Tom Peters, Zig Ziglar, Kenneth Blanchard, and Billy Graham, to name a few. They are people who have presented powerful messages in response to people's needs. And they've related valuable information and insights to satisfy those needs. You can, too.

There are times when the challenges of presenting are tantamount to "it's a dirty job but somebody's got to do it." But for the trained and skilled presenter it's an exciting job, and you're glad to be one of those doing it. It's gratifying, and stimulating, and invigorating, and rewarding to be a person of influence. And good presenters do influence.

The good news is that effective presenters are perceived to be different. When you acquire and refine the skills of presenting in a way that has an impact on people, others see you as different from the norm. Skilled presenting is a distinguishing characteristic. It conveys personal confidence and professional competence. Whether or not that's true, in fact, is a moot point. People perceive it to be true.

From my own experience, I can tell you I've often role-played the part of a presenter. In fact, my stomach may have been twisted in knots. But when you play the role often enough over time, you become the role that you play. So it is with presenting. The people who were passed over for promotion yesterday because they were perceived to be lacking in confidence can be the people who are advanced tomorrow—when they become presenters with pizzazz!

The good news is that as the volume, complexity, and demands for information increase, so too will the demands for skilled presenters. At a time when more information is available to us than ever before, there is a growing need for people who can sort through, select, and disseminate information effectively. No one is better equipped to perform those tasks than people with good presentation skills. They have the very abilities needed in an information society: the abilities to organize data, communicate ideas, and develop creative ways to give meaning to the many, many messages.

The best news is that anyone can learn to present effectively. Like any other task, it's just a matter of developing a set of skills and practicing them to proficiency. Even the dreaded fear of public speaking can be overcome with proven techniques. The secret lies in understanding and practicing presentations that embody the "right things."

Effective Presentations Are Balanced and Satisfy Four Basic Criteria

The spoken language takes on greater meaning when we clothe it in visual imagery. Poets have understood this for centuries. So, too, did the originator of the phrase, "A picture is worth a thousand words."

Here's a word picture for you. Imagine you're a gymnast performing on the balance beam. That beam is a mere four inches across. It's about

Figure 1-1.

the same width as a street curb or a single railroad tie. If you're going to walk along it steadily, you need to step with care.

Next time you're in front of a group, recall that imagery. Picture Olga Korbutt or Mary Lou Retton, Olympic gold-medal gymnasts. Your objective when you present is the same as theirs: to go for the gold. The way you win is to keep your performance in balance.

What does this have to do with presenting? Presenting is a balancing act. On one side of the beam is the information in your presentation; on the other side are relational elements. Lean too far one way or the other, and the results are less than effective. As your effectiveness diminishes, so too does your ability to persuade. Olympic gymnasts don't persuade judges to award them the gold if they lose their balance when they present. Neither will you. Your audience is your judge. And they respond most favorably to a well-balanced presentation.

Another way to think of presenting: it's like balancing on a "Bongo Board." When I used this illustration recently in a workshop, I realized I'm older than I feel. Half the people in the group didn't know what a Bongo Board was! (I was once again reminded of the importance of choosing examples that are relevant to the audience.) If you don't recall or don't know what a Bongo Board is, picture a miniature surfboard placed atop a small cylindrical drum, as shown in Figure 1-1.

When you present, imagine that you're perched midway atop the board. One side represents the information you're presenting; the other side, the way you relate to the audience. Staying in balance between the two is essential to an effective presentation. Easy to do? Not if you haven't done it before. And not if you haven't learned some tricks of the trade.

The first "trade secret" is the criteria a presentation should satisfy. You can remember them using the mnemonic device AMMA. Meaning "Amma (I'm a) good presenter!"

A	Attention-getting
M	Meaningful
M	Memorable
A	Activating

An effective presentation gets and keeps attention. It is meaningful and memorable for the audience. And it moves people to act on the message they've received.

Notice the last criterion is activating, not motivating. Motivational speeches abound. But measurements of people's galvanic skin responses show the motivation is typically short-lived.

The electrical energy our bodies emit is understandably higher during or immediately after a motivational event. Some of the factors that contribute to this increased energy output include the excitement generated by a group, getting oriented to a different and upbeat environment, and anticipating the guest speaker. We feel "hyped," as the saying goes.

But what happens when people return to their customary surroundings and resume their day-to-day routines? That's right. Their responses return to normal. The heightened energy we understood to be motivation declines as people return to their usual activities.

The challenge for a presenter, then, is not just to motivate. (I'm not interested solely in raising energy output.) It is, rather, to activate. An effective presenter aims at increasing understanding and influencing the way people think and feel and behave. In that way, an audience is more likely to be moved to follow through and take the action proposed in a presentation.

Activating people occurs much more readily when the first three criteria are satisfied. It stands to reason that when you've maintained people's attention and presented a message that's meaningful and memorable for them, they'll be more inclined to act on it in response.

Keep these four criteria in mind. They guide the way you prepare your presentation, how you relate it to your audience, and the manner in which you deliver it for optimum affect.

Whenever you're getting ready to present, ask yourself:

What will get and keep this audience's attention?
How can I make my message more meaningful and memorable for them?
What will move them to act on what I present?

You'll discover some techniques for answering these questions in the chapters that follow.

To Present Like a Pro, Remember

- Principles to bear in mind:

  The purpose of presenting is to persuade.
  Perception is more powerful than fact.
  People are inundated with data.
  People forget fast.
  Effective presentations are balanced.

- Effective presentations satisfy these four criteria:

  A   Attention-getting
  M   Meaningful
  M   Memorable
  A   Activating

References

1. Jay Conrad Levinson, *Guerilla Marketing,* Houghton Mifflin, Boston, 1984, p. 26.
2. Harvey L. Poppel, "Managerial/Professional Productivity," *Outlook,* Booz-Allen & Hamilton, Fall-Winter 1980.

2

Preparing Your Message

You've been asked to present a report at a senior management meeting Friday morning. Secretly, you harbor mixed feelings. On the one hand, this is a great opportunity! On the other hand, you dread being up on your feet in front of that group. And you're not thrilled about the extra work it's going to take to get ready.

Well, no time like the present to get started. You grab a yellow tablet, poise your pencil over it, and begin to write:

> Good morning, ladies and gentlemen. I'm Terry Jones, customer service manager of the marketing department. I want to thank you for the time...

No, no. That's all wrong. Not enough oomph!

Your phone rings. Great! Just the excuse you need to set your tablet aside. Besides, you need more time to think about what you're going to say, and your presentation is still a few days away.

Later (too late), there you are hunched over the dining room table at home, scrambling to get ready for your presentation the next day. "Good morning..." You try the line out, aloud this time, with emphasis. Doesn't sound right. Panic sets in as you realize this isn't going to come off the way you want.

Sound familiar? Unless you're a veteran presenter, you've had an experience very like this—or you will when you get a chance to present. If this presenting business is supposed to be so terrific, why is it sometimes so difficult to get started? What do you do?

First, you recognize that presenting isn't the same as talking. You don't just calm your fears, jump to your feet, and read your written report aloud. Although we've all witnessed speakers who do just that, it's not what a persuasive presenter does.

Presenting is more like narrating your own book, with style. Before you can narrate it you have to write it. You have to give thought to your central theme and how to develop it. You have to consider who your readers will be before you begin. In other words, you have to prepare.

Like books, presentations take a variety of forms. They occur in many different settings as well. You may have the enviable opportunity of presenting a long-awaited new product to an eager sales force. You may have the unenviable task of announcing a policy or corporate decision that you know is going to be unpopular with the troops. You may be asked to make a presentation on a highly controversial subject or to speak at a service club meeting on a topic of your choice. You may present to a board meeting of upper-level executives, to your own group of employees, or to an audience that includes the general public.

Before You Present

Regardless of the subject or setting, one thing remains consistently true. The most effective presenters are prepared. They've determined, in advance, what information to present and how to deliver it so that it's well received.

I emphasize *in advance*. Even so-called extemporaneous speakers prepare ahead of time. (According to Webster's: *extemporaneous* is "carefully prepared but delivered without notes.") As one writer observed, "Mark Twain, the great American orator, said, 'It takes three weeks to prepare a good impromptu speech.'"[1] A presentation will lack focus and order if you fail ahead of time to sort through your thoughts, and extract and organize key points from what might be volumes of source materials.

That's not to imply that presenting is difficult or time-consuming. At least, it doesn't need to be. In fact, it can be quite easy. It will come naturally to you when you use the "tools of the trade" and become proficient with them.

The tools you'll become acquainted with here have helped novices and veterans alike. I've introduced them to managers, salespeople, attorneys, architects, and business students from various career fields. In every case, their response has been, "This made it so much easier!" Follow these simple guidelines and you'll avoid those last-ditch, late-into-the-night efforts at drafting a presentation. Once the pressure's off, you can turn presenting into a pleasure.

When you prepare, reflect on the principles and criteria covered in Chapter 1. The presentation you'll be delivering is one among hundreds of others that people will hear. So you should ask yourself, "How do I ensure that mine will have a positive impact?"

Your presentation will have impact when your message "speaks" to the hearts and minds of your listeners—when it's meaningful and memorable for the particular audience you're going to address. That means making decisions at two stages in order to accomplish an "M & M" presentation. First, what approach are you going to take to present your subject? Next, how will you structure your message?

Which Approach?

To land a plane at any major metropolitan airport, a pilot may take one of several approaches. Which approach is the best one? The decision is based on numerous factors: other aircraft traffic in the area, weather conditions, conditions on the ground, sometimes an emergency situation on the plane. But no one approach is used all the time. Alternate avenues of arriving at the destination enable the pilot to adapt to varying circumstances.

There's a difference between a pilot steering a plane on its approach, and you "steering" the course of a presentation. The pilot receives instructions from an air traffic controller. You have to make the decisions yourself. You're the "controller" of your presentation. As such, you need to consider the different approaches you can use to bring your audience to its destination (your objective). And remember: No one approach applies in all situations.

Many speakers fall into a common trap. They approach a subject from a single point of view: theirs. After all, it's your presentation. You're an expert on the subject. You have a wealth of information that you've researched carefully. You're enthused about what you have to say.

Now, what about your audience? Sad, but true: they may not care. At least not at the outset of your presentation. They may be there out of curiosity or on demand. They may be preoccupied. They may view the information from a different point of view. They may not share the same degree of interest in the subject. (Of course, that's one of your purposes in presenting: to persuade them to.)

For whatever reasons an audience may not be with you at the outset, you can win them over. To do so, you need to deliver your message from their point of view. Your presentation doesn't need to be meaningful to you. You already know the meaning of your message. It needs to be made meaningful to them. One way to do that is by altering your approach. How you approach your subject depends primarily on the nature of your audience.

Know Your Customer

Textbooks refer to gaining insight into your listeners as "audience analysis." I call it "knowing your customer." The word *analysis* conjures up images of an in-depth research effort and scares people off like the plague. Consequently, too many presenters don't give their listeners a second thought, much less a first one.

"Knowing your customer" is a different matter. It's understanding who you're dealing with so you know how to serve up a presentation that appeals to them, a presentation that they'll "buy." Understanding the people you're going to address and delivering your message in relevant terms are essential to being a persuasive presenter.

In the case of presenters, the "customer" varies. Generally, an audience is a composite of people, a "corporate" body, a group. On one occasion you may present to five people, on another, to fifty or five hundred. Nevertheless, most audiences are composed of people who are "predominantly."

Members of an audience are predominantly male or female; predominantly young or mature; predominantly business executives, or government clerks, or homemakers, or citizens with special interests. It's important to take the predominant characteristics of your audience into account, because people of different types respond to the same things in different ways.

It's also important to understand the setting. Setting refers to the overall environment, the context in which your presentation will occur. It's also a factor that influences how you'll present.

Knowing the audience and the setting helps determine the approach you ought to take, both to your subject and with respect to the overall "presence" you want to create. For example, suppose you're asked to make presentations on the general topic of time management. Your presentation in a formal setting to mature, conservative corporate executives will differ from the one you make to business students attending a casual weekend retreat.

This example isn't meant to label people. It is meant to alert presenters to the importance of considering the way a topic is approached. The same approach will not be equally effective in different settings, with people of different gender or occupations, who have different expectations and reasons for being there. The best presentations are those that customize the approach to the "customer."

The responses to one presentation I observed reinforce this point.

The speech was delivered at a community business conference. The guest speaker was the director of training and education for a multinational corporation, and he was introduced with a list of impressive credentials. He spoke on the subject of employee training.

As his presentation unfolded, it became apparent he didn't know his audience. It was composed, predominantly, of owners and managers of local businesses. U.S. Small Business Administration figures indicated that eighty percent of the businesses in that area have five or fewer employees.

The speaker talked about training budgets in the millions of dollars, probably more than his average listener grossed in five years. He talked about sophisticated program and curriculum development spanning months of effort and dozens of employees. He talked about ergonomically designed classrooms. (I'd surmise half his audience didn't know what *ergonomic* meant.) He talked about everything except what was meaningful and memorable to his audience.

The responses were predictable. To my right, a gentleman began scribbling a "To Do" list. To my left, another nodded off. And all around, you could see folks glancing at their watches or shifting restlessly in their seats. When he was finished, the customary applause was noticeably unenthused.

That the audience responded unfavorably was not the fault of the topic. It was a relevant topic that the entrepreneurs and managers attending the conference needed to hear about. But they needed to hear about it in a way to which they could relate. The fault lay, not with the topic, but with a presenter who failed to "know the customer" and failed to adjust his approach accordingly.

Approaching your subject from the audience's point of view is a first and essential step. It influences the points you'll make, the terminology you'll use, and the illustrations and examples you'll bring into play. So even before you outline your presentation, consider the nature of the audience. Imagine yourself seated on their side of the desk, the conference room, the theater platform, or classroom. Imagine listening to you from their perspective.

The answers to the questions that follow will give you valuable insights on an audience and help you determine what approach to take. They provide basic demographics, literally speaking, "a picture of the people."

A Snapshot of the Audience

Consider the following characteristics when you think about your listeners.

Gender.   What gender will I be addressing: predominantly male or female?

Age.   What age group will I be speaking to: predominantly youngsters, teens, young adults, mature, middle-aged, or seniors?

Occupation and Profession.   What occupations or professions are represented, and at what level? Private industry, corporate, entrepreneurial, government, education, legal, medical, homemaking, community service, public-interest associations, what...? Will I be addressing executives, senior or junior management, employees, self-employed people, or the unemployed?

Educational Level.   Are members of this audience college-educated, high school graduates, or less educated? Are they highly scholastic in their attitudes or more down to earth?

Setting.   You might think the setting is one of the logistics of presenting you can take care of when you get there. Not so. It does, in fact, have an effect on the nature of your audience. People behave and respond differently in audiences of one thousand than they do in small groups of five or ten. A presentation that works in a smaller, more intimate setting may not work in an auditorium. You want to understand as much as you can about the setting before you prepare your presentation.

Will you be presenting in a convention center theater, conference room, classroom, or office? What's the size of the audience? What's the expected or preferred style in this setting: formal, informal, or intimate? Will you be presenting from behind a podium, on an open platform, or moving among the group? What audiovisual equipment will be available?

Mood and Expectations.   Depending on the nature of the presentation event, the audience will have formed certain expectations. They may be receptive to hearing one kind of message but not another. For example, what a group of salespeople will be inclined to sit through during a two-day product training session is far different from what they're predisposed to hear at a two-day sales convention. (That's party time!)

In some situations, the purpose of the meeting is very clear. You know what's expected and what the mood will be. It will be serious or social, intense or light-hearted, or something in between. In cases where the mood and expectations aren't clear to you, ask: "What outcome do you want to achieve? What will be the prevailing mood?"

Tailoring the Message

Once you've identified the predominant characteristics of the audience and the setting, ask yourself: What will appeal to them? What will this group of people consider important? What material will be meaningful and memorable for my listeners in these circumstances?

Imagine if that conference speaker who spoke on employee training had had the answers to these questions beforehand. He would have known to approach his subject from a different angle (or at least I'd hope so). The audience would have been much more receptive. He might even have received a round of resounding applause in response!

Getting Started

Once you've determined the approach to your subject, you're ready to develop the content of your message. From what I've observed, this is a point where many people get hung up. It's the reason preparation is often put off until the very last minute.

It's understandable if you start by staring at a blank sheet of paper. Suddenly, you cast yourself in the role of the author of the next great American novel. You suffer a siege of writer's block. That is obviously not the way to start. So, what is?

Worksheets

In the appendix of this book you'll find worksheets designed to make it easier to develop a presentation. I recommend that presenters start with a copy of these worksheets at hand. Using these worksheets is like giving your battery a jump start when your car engine is stalled. Once you have some help getting started, you gain momentum as you go along.

On the pages that follow, we'll go step by step through a model outline for preparing a presentation. Many or all of the components may sound familiar, especially if you've presented before. What's new and improved is not the components but the manner in which you develop them.

As you prepare the content of your message, structure the information in an orderly and logical manner. In that way, you make it easier for people to follow, digest, and retain what you're saying to them. If the audience has difficulty following your train of thought, your message won't get and keep their attention. If it doesn't get and keep their attention, it can't be meaningful, memorable, or activating. In other words, it won't satisfy the criteria of an effective presentation.

At the same time, you want this whole business of preparing a presentation made easier for you. A lot easier! So what do you do to accomplish this?

Prepare in Stages

Prepare your message in stages. Don't sit down and attempt to write the whole presentation in one sitting. The only time you need to do that is if you're called on to speak extemporaneously. Then you quickly create a mental outline. But extemporaneous speaking is the exception, not the rule. In most cases, you should have sufficient lead time to develop a presentation in increments. Approach the task of preparing your material in three stages:

1. Outline each component.
2. Develop the narrative.
3. Design supplemental materials (audiovisuals, handouts).

A fourth stage, of course, would be to practice. But that occurs after your presentation is prepared.

Building a presentation is like building a house. You build it in stages. The outline is your blueprint. Developing the narrative furnishes the interior. And the supplemental materials are the exterior touches (like landscaping). They're designed to enhance the structure, and they're done last.

The way you plan and build a house differs from the way in which you live in it. A presentation is similar: you prepare the material in one order and deliver it in another. For example, when delivered, every presentation begins with an introductory opener. But that's not the place to begin when you prepare. As the following outlines indicate, you prepare the components of a presentation in one order and present them in another.

Prepare in This Order

1. Your objective
2. Key points with supporting material and transitions
3. Preview and summary
4. Opener
5. Closing "to do"

Present in This Order

Introduction
    Opener
        Objective
        Preview
Body
    Key Point 1
        Supporting material
        Transition
    Key Point 2
        Supporting material
        Transition
    Key Point 3
        Supporting material
Closing
    Summary
    "To do"

The remainder of this chapter explores in detail each component in the order in which a presentation is prepared.

If you have a specific presentation in mind as you're reading this, you might outline some notes for it as we go along. In that way, you'll discover (by hands-on application) just how easy it is to use this approach to preparing. And, you'll end up with a tangible result that will give you a sense of satisfaction.

Prepare the Objective

With a blank worksheet copied from the appendix or yellow pad in hand, write a brief statement that answers the question:

> "What do I want to accomplish by delivering this presentation?"

That's your objective. It is, simply, the object of presenting. It's the purpose, the aim, the target of your presentation, the outcome you want to achieve. When you've achieved it, you can shout, "Bull's eye!"

The objective is the first element you prepare because all of the rest of your presentation is designed to support it. In fact, a good rule of thumb to follow when developing your presentation is this:

> If it doesn't support the objective, don't do it.

Have you ever walked out of a presentation given by someone else, thinking, "What in the world was that all about?" The presenter may have been a dynamic speaker. The visual aids may have been colorful or amusing. The subject may have been one that, by its title, interested you. But if you can't describe the intent of the message and you don't know what you're supposed to do with it, the presentation lacked an objective.

One approach to formulating a very clear-cut statement of your objective is to think in these terms:

> By the conclusion of this presentation people will _____ (what?).

Stating an objective in this way focuses attention on what you want your audience to do with your message. A presentation typically is aimed at getting people to:

Understand something, or

Be able to do something, or

Do it.

For example, do you want your audience to understand the benefits of your proposal? be able to use your proposal? or buy ("buy into," approve, accept, adopt) your proposal?

Which level of objective you choose depends on the purpose your presentation is intended to serve and the time you have available. A fifteen-minute motivational message given at a management meeting might have as an objective, "They'll understand how important they are to the organization." A day's management training session, on the other hand, may have as an objective, "They'll be able to write a performance plan."

To cite a more specific example: Suppose you were making a presentation on the subject of presentation skills. Your objective might be stated as any one of the following: "By the conclusion of this presentation, the audience will...

1. Understand the principles of persuasive presentations, or

2. Be able to develop a well-organized presentation following the model outline, or

3. Do a presentation that is attention-getting, meaningful, memorable, and activating."

In a sales-oriented situation, the third form of objective might specify something like this: "By the conclusion of this presentation, the audience will buy a copy of this book to give to a friend."

Formulating an achievable and clearly stated objective is crucial. From the outset it provides a focus for preparation and guides you in determining what to include in the body of your message.

Stating the objective when you present is equally important. Doing so lets your audience know what to expect. It readies them for what they're about to hear. However, when you deliver your presentation, the objective would be stated in more conversational terms in relation to the audience. For example, it might be said like this: "Today, we'll explore some of the advantages of becoming a more effective presenter."

Earlier, I compared building a presentation to building a house. When you define your objective, you lay the foundation.

Objective

The Foundation

Prepare Key Points

With the foundation in place, you're ready to go on and outline the body of your presentation. Begin by identifying the one, two, or three key points you'll make in order to achieve your objective. Key points are those that "unlock the door" to your subject. They let the audience in on the most important content areas of your message.

Notice I specified "one, two, or three." It's been said that every great message contains at least one but not more than three key points. The rule of three should be applied to every presentation you make. It forces you to think through your material and distill the most significant points. It provides a structure for grouping information into organized categories. And it enables you to communicate your message with more clarity for your listeners.

The Rule of Three

Why the rule of three? There are several reasons, all related to delivering a presentation that keeps attention and that's easy to remember. If you'll recall the principles for presenters related in Chapter 1, people are inundated with data and quick to forget. One way to increase what they'll remember from you is:

```
                              KISS
                    Keep It Simple, Speaker!
```

Three or fewer key points keeps it simple for your listeners. They'll be able to retain more of less.

Consider how we codify information. Did you ever notice how we remember things in groups of threes and fours? When someone asks your telephone number, you answer with a set of three numbers and a second set of four: 123-1234. The way we store and recall this information represents the brain's effort to organize and combine data, making it easier to remember. Instead of remembering seven separate digits of a phone number, we have to deal only with one group of three and one group of four.

The same principle applies to the body of your presentation. Think about speakers you've heard who rambled endlessly, stringing together one idea after another, on and on and on. This is a "shopping list" style of presenting. It results when a presenter doesn't take the time to organize the information or decides to "walk 'em through the whole store and let 'em pick out what they want."

The list approach isn't very effective. It assumes the audience is interested and listening, which they may not be if you don't make it easy for them. You run the risk of leaving the audience with the impression that your thoughts are disjointed. They may perceive that you lack the confidence and expertise to identify and recommend what's most important.

Perhaps more to the point, how much do you think people remember afterward of a shopping list? Imagine making up a grocery list of thirty items. When you get to the store, you realize you left the list at home. How many of the items will you remember? By comparison, imagine making up a list of just three: dairy, produce, and meats. Although you're still not likely to remember everything, you'll remember at least those three.

If you've ever attended a hit-and-run seminar, you're familiar with the shopping list approach. A seminar company flies a presenter into town, advertises an agenda that runs from 9 a.m. to 4 p.m., and offers 149 ideas for self-improvement. (If you've been to one, you know I'm not exaggerating.) At 4:15, the audience is on its way out, exclaiming, "Boy, that was great!" They're hyped! Two days later (if it takes that long), they remember very little except perhaps the color of the speaker's suit or a new business contact made during lunch.

If you want your presentation remembered, follow the rule of three. It doesn't mean you'll always have three points. There may be times when you'll have only two; and in exceptional cases, you'll have four. The real importance of focusing on the rule of three is that it produces a better presentation. It disciplines a presenter to prepare—to clarify and organize the content. It provides the audience with a message they'll be better able to assimilate and retain.

How do you determine the one, two, or three key points you want to make? Consider two questions.

What points will best lead to my objective?

What points do I most want the audience to remember?

Again, using the example of the topic of presentation skills, the outline developed so far might look like this:

Objective: By the conclusion of this presentation, people will understand how to present like a PRO.

Key Point 1: Prepare.

Key Point 2: Relate.

Key Point 3: Optimize.

A Sequence That's Easy to Follow

An effective presentation guides listeners through an orderly sequence that makes it easy for them to follow, digest, and retain the message. So once you've decided on your key points, put them in some kind of logical sequence. There are various schemes you can use.

Chronological Order.   Key points can be presented chronologically—in the order that they occur in time. Depending on the subject, they would advance from (1) past to (2) present to (3) future, or (1) the first step to (2) the second step to (3) the third step.

Spatial Arrangement.   Key points can be related by area. For example, a presentation on national sales performance would be arranged in order of results in the East, the Midwest, and the West. If your company has four regions—Eastern, Central, Southern, and Western—apply the exception, rather than the rule, and use four key points.

Topical Approach.   If your message doesn't lend itself to being organized by time or space, try a topical approach. With this approach, a well-ordered sequence occurs by advancing your listeners from (1) the least important point to (2) the more important to (3) the point of greatest significance. Relate last the point you want remembered most.

Concerns and Solutions.   Presentations regarding solutions to problems may be organized under two key points, concerns and solutions. (Avoid using the word *problem* as in *problems and solutions*. People don't like to be reminded that they have problems. *Concerns* and *needs* are more palatable words.) You would then outline the concerns and solutions in not more than three key subpoints, using one of the schemes noted above.

In the sample outline on presentation skills noted earlier, the key points are organized in chronological order. They proceed from the first step, to the second, to the last. It so happens they're also arranged to take advantage of a mnemonic device.

"Labels" That Are Easy to Remember

Mnemonic devices help people remember. The first letter of each key point outlined in the earlier example spell *PRO* (Prepare, Relate, Op-

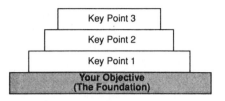

Figure 2-1. The Framework of a Presentation

timize). It's an acronym, a mnemonic device that serves to jog people's memory.

In one presentation on the value of reducing the costs of business, the speaker used the acronym LOW to identify his three key points. The letters stood for Lean and mean, Overtime, and Winning edge. That I remember the points months later speaks to the value of acronyms.

Another common mnemonic is to begin each key point with the same letter or word. In one presentation I make, I address the three Cs of customer service: Courtesy, Care, and handling Complaints.

Key points are the highlights of your presentation. You know the audience won't remember everything you say. But if they remember nothing else, you want them to walk away with at least your key points in mind. So take care to select the points that have the most meaning. Arrange them in an order that helps the audience follow them. And if you can label your key points using a mnemonic device, do so if it makes sense (i.e., reflects the theme of your presentation).

If your key points are listed in an order that develops your message logically, you now have the framework in place for a well-designed structure (as depicted in Figure 2-1). Each key point represents an additional story to the building, moving your "visitors" naturally from one stage of your presentation to the next.

One final factor in determining the sequence of key points is that of impact. Like a symphony, your presentation should build to a crescendo! Arrange your points to lead to an exciting or forceful conclusion.

Prepare Supporting Material

The framework of a structure won't hold up without supports. Neither will your presentation. So the next component you outline is material that will clearly communicate and substantiate your key points.

What will convince people to accept your key points? Sufficient evidence alone is not enough, as any trial attorney will tell you. The evidence must be relevant to the subject and meaningful and memorable for the audience. It must be developed to convince and persuade.

Sources

Supporting material can come from a variety of sources.

Internal.   There's ample information available within most organizations. Product descriptions, performance statistics, newsletters, and all kinds of reports are sources for supporting material. With as much paperwork as companies generate these days, you probably have access to ample evidence right in your own office.

External.   Business, industry, and trade journals, newspaper articles, and books are all sources for supporting material. In addition, computerized database services offer virtually unlimited access to information on any subject.

Personal.   Don't overlook supporting material that resides within your own experience. There are times when you can appropriately, and most meaningfully, substantiate a key point with personal insights, anecdotes, or examples.

One of the advantages to living in an information-rich society is the ease with which you can locate an abundance of supporting material. Unless you're delivering a technical presentation that requires very specific evidence, you probably have a wealth of information on hand from sources to which you are routinely exposed.

The trick lies in exposing yourself to information. For anyone who presents regularly, I recommend daily reading of your local newspaper and a major national newspaper. Subscribe to—and at least scan—major business or trade publications. Read books in your subject area that are currently popular and nonfiction that appears on the best-seller list. (Those are titles and authors most audiences will be familiar with.) Watch television programs related to your subject area, notably those with a news journal format and documentaries.

Set up a simple filing system with hanging folders or an accordion-style file box. Whenever you come across information that might lend itself to being used as supporting material, cut it out and file it away. The next time you present, you'll be amazed at how much material you have at your fingertips: good examples, quotable quotes, illustrations, current statistics. You'll save a lot of the time and effort you'd otherwise spend researching and compiling material.

Types of Supporting Material

As you check out your sources of supporting material, consider the different types of evidence that are most appropriate to the subject, the audience, and the setting. Material that will substantiate your key points may occur in any of the following forms.

- Examples
- Comparisons
- Quotations
- Findings
- Audiovisual media

Examples.   Examples provide experiential, qualitative support. They demonstrate that a general point is true or correct by describing a specific person or event. Suppose I stated the key point, "Skillful presenting advances careers." I could relate, "For example, Tom Peters has achieved considerable success as a result of his ability to present."

An effective form of example is a verbal illustration, a "word picture" of what has, or could, occur. It's effective in that it prompts the audience to visualize a situation that exemplifies your key point. In effect, they mentally participate in it. (When preparing a verbal illustration, you might remember this marketing precept: It doesn't have to be true, just believable.)

Comparisons.   Comparisons provide support that clarifies or amplifies. When a point is compared to something with which the audience is familiar, they're more likely to understand it. Understanding it, they're generally more receptive to accepting it.

Years ago I presented training sessions on the use of word processing equipment. In those days, there were more than a few secretaries who demonstrated resistance to this change. They wanted nothing to do with a new-fangled approach to typing. A presenter who asserted the key point "easy to use" couldn't assume it would be accepted on the presenter's authority alone. But comparing functions of the equipment to the familiar typewriter made the message more convincing.

When a direct comparison isn't available, try using an analogy. An analogy contends that if two things are alike in one respect, they'll be alike in other respects as well. An analogy operates on this premise: If A and B are similar and you accept this is true of A, then it stands to reason you'll accept it's also true of B.

When I present seminars on salesmanship, I draw an analogy between selling and courtship. The analogy creates a framework for describing the sales process that's familiar to my listeners, that persuades the audience of the importance of relational skills, and that offers opportunities for humor as well.

A contrast (in contrast to comparisons) presents points in opposition to one another. The differences are highlighted. In that respect, contrasts can be an effective means for amplifying points in a presentation. A newspaper article presented evidence in support of building more jails by the use of contrasting data. In the same sentence, a 337 percent increase in crime was contrasted with a 27 percent increase in prison construction. When high and low, black and white, sweet and sour are juxtaposed, the contrast can have a startling, and very convincing, effect.

Quotations.   Quotations provide support on the basis of authority or celebrity. We are a nation of hero-worshippers. Many people conclude, "If he or she said it, it must be true." A quotation gives you the benefit of some authority's "truth."

Ever notice how company presentations (like a corporate prospectus or sales proposal) include a list of clients and testimonials? They are intended to support the company's claims and the proposal they're presenting. It's a way of saying, "In case you don't believe me, you can certainly believe them." Of course, citing testimonials from the executives of Fortune 100 companies has more credibility than citing unknowns. Similarly, quotations from experts on a subject provide greater support than the opinion of someone whose name won't be recognized.

Findings.   Findings supply quantitative evidence in the form of reports, research results, or statistics. Data is used to validate a point, to persuade the audience to come to the same conclusion you're presenting based on the "facts."

While it's essential to supply factual material in support of a presentation, doing so should be approached with two cautions in mind. For one, be sure the data is current and accurate. We live in a fast-changing society. More research and fact-gathering is going on today than ever before. In some fields, what was found to be true six months ago is obsolete today. The more technical the presentation and the more informed the audience is about your subject, the more important it is to be sure your facts are correct and that your sources are reliable.

The second caution is this: Don't rely on facts alone. Marketing studies have found that people respond first on the basis of feelings. They then consider the facts in order to validate their feelings, to have a "logical" basis that justifies their response. The primacy of feelings explains the importance of relational skills (the subject of Chapter 3).

Audiovisual Media.   Audiovisual media provide vocal or graphic support for the types of material described above. Audiovisuals are discussed further in Chapter 5.

Balance

If there's one quality that characterizes an effective presentation, it's balance. When you consider what supporting material to use, look for a balance among internal, external, and personal sources and among the various types of material outlined above. Relating only examples from personal experience won't provide sufficient evidence. Relating only facts from internal sources won't provide sufficient evidence. A combination of sources and types, used in balance, will produce the most persuasive presentation.

How and How Much

Supporting material accounts for most of the content of a presentation. In that respect, it generally takes the most time to identify, collect, and develop. At this preliminary stage of preparing an outline, you want to avoid getting stalled doing research or trying to be creative. Just outline some ideas. Make a few notes about material you have in mind or evidence you want to find. Later, when you compose the narrative of your presentation, you can more fully develop the supporting material.

In many cases, finding and developing the material can be delegated to someone else. If a secretary or administrative staff person is available, he or she may be able to do some of the legwork for you. The notes you've made on the model outline will serve to guide them.

How extensively you develop supporting material depends on a number of factors. Time is the most pertinent deciding factor. Obviously, you would prepare less material less extensively for a fifteen-minute speech than you would for a full day's seminar.

Setting is another deciding factor. If you'll be presenting in an interactive setting, determine how much time to present versus how much time to allow for audience participation. Even in more formal settings where the presenter does all the speaking, you need to determine how much time, if any, you'll allow for questions and answers at the end.

Avoid the temptation to use too much supporting material. Keep the rule of three in mind. If you present too much material to support your key points, you'll end up with a shopping list. The significant points will get lost in a maze of rambling data. Conversely, too little material may not be sufficient to substantiate your points, and your presentation won't be convincing.

Once the supporting material is outlined, you're ready to make note of the last component in the body of your presentation: transitions. (And that's a transition statement.)

Prepare Transitions

Transitions act like stairways in the presentation you're building. They step listeners from one key point to the next. They are minute pieces of a presentation, but they are very critical. Transitions help your listeners stay with you, making your message easier to follow and remember.

As the presenter, you know when you're moving on—when you're stepping off the first floor and proceeding to the second. But your audience doesn't. Without transitions, you could be halfway into your next point. Meanwhile, some of your listeners are trying to figure out what this has to do with what you were talking about before. Afterward, the overall impression they may have is that your presentation was incomplete or confusing.

Transitions help keep the audience on track. They also serve to bring the audience back. If some people have mentally wandered elsewhere, a transition can regain their attention. It alerts people that your message is advancing.

There's no excuse for a presenter to overlook transitions, since they're so simple to devise. A transition is simply a statement that acts as a minisummary and minipreview within the body of a presentation. It announces the end of one point and introduces the next.

A transition statement stepped us out of the previous section and into this one. Other transition phrases would include statements like these:

"Having considered x, let's go on and look at y."

"In addition to results in the East, we've enjoyed remarkable success in the Midwest."

And here's another. Having developed the objective and the body of your presentation, you're ready to outline the preview and summary.

Prepare the Preview and Summary

Preparing your preview and summary is easy. Just encapsulate your one, two, or three key points in brief sentence form. For example, the preview to the presentation of this chapter stated: "That means making decisions at two stages. First, what approach are you going to take to present your subject? Next, how will you structure your message?" The key points are "approach" and "structure." (You can imagine how the summary will read.)

You'll recall that one of the criteria for an effective presentation is that it's memorable for your listeners. If people don't remember what you said, your objective won't be achieved. If your objective isn't achieved, you're not having the impact and influence you could be having on people.

Most trainers are well acquainted with the importance of previewing and summarizing a message. They apply the formula T × 3:

Preview	T-1: Tell them what you're going to tell them.
Body	T-2: Tell them.
Summary	T-3: Tell them what you told them.

It's a formula that applies not only to training situations, but on all occasions when you're presenting to people. It's one of the techniques that helps people recall the highlights of your message.

Add to that one of the principles of persuasion: People are most readily persuaded by what they hear frequently and recently. Preview your key points, state them during the body of your message and then reiterate them in the summary. When you do, you satisfy both your intent for the audience to remember and your purpose to persuade.

How Does It Look?

You've almost finished building your presentation. The preview serves as a window into your message that gives the audience an advance view

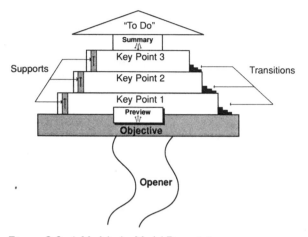

Figure 2-2. A Model of a Model Presentation

of the key points. The summary is like looking back from the attic, reminding the audience of where they've been. All that remains to complete the structure (as illustrated in Figure 2-2) is to prepare an inviting entrance and a closing that caps it all off.

Prepare the Opener

Every presentation begins with an introductory opener. Some you hear are good. Others are not so good. Obviously, you want to prepare an opener that's going to be good, one that will entice peof e to listen to you.

Think of the opener not in terms of what begins your presentation but in terms of what will open up the audience. When you concentrate on opening up the audience, they'll be more receptive to you and to your message. What opens people up is what gets their attention right at the outset.

The opener invites the audience to come in and listen to more. As such, it's one of the more important elements of your presentation. It should capture people's attention and foreshadow your theme. To accomplish both may take some creativity. Developing an original and meaningful opener can take some time and thought. For that reason, wait to prepare the opener until after you've outlined the body of your presentation.

Types of Openers

What types of openers invite people's attention? Any one of these will do, provided they're well chosen and well stated.

- Authoritative quotation
- Rhetorical question
- Declarative statement
- Scenario
- Anecdote

The following examples illustrate each form. For the sake of consistency, we'll stay with the subject of presentation skills.

Authoritative Quotation.   This opener begins with a quotation:

> "Leadership is the quality that transforms good intentions into positive action."[2] That's the observation of T. Boone Pickens, Jr., founder of America's largest independent oil company and one of this country's foremost business leaders. Today, you'll discover how to demonstrate your qualities of leadership through the vehicle of skillful presenting.

Quotations work best when they're from someone who's a recognized authority on the subject. Just quoting someone doesn't gain attention. When it comes to having impact with quotations, it's who you know, not what you know. So the "who" you quote should be an attention-getter. Well-known celebrities, politicians, authors, and leaders in their fields will all do. If you're not sure the name will be recognized by your audience, state the source's authority. In the example cited above, the person quoted gains authority (and your presentation gains credibility) when he's described as "one of this country's foremost business leaders."

Rhetorical Question.   "When public speaking has been described as our number one fear, why would anyone want to learn how to do it?"

A rhetorical question invites attention because it involves the audience in your presentation right from the start. When you open by posing a question, people's minds shift into gear as they mentally digest the question and formulate a response.

A rhetorical question is even better if it appeals to people's natural curiosity. The response you want to trigger is something like this: "I don't know. Why would they?" And the audience is motivated to listen to you for the answer.

Declarative Statement.   "Training is a multibillion-dollar industry in this country, and it's a market that's growing rapidly every day. For the individual who presents skillfully, that means a lot of opportunity."

   A declarative statement makes a bold, emphatic statement of fact. To be attention-getting, it needs to address an issue that's of interest to the audience, one that will raise their level of expectation or concern. To be effective, it needs to be delivered expressively. A declarative statement that's stated without a tone of voice and facial expression that give meaning to the declaration will fail to have the impact on your listeners that an opener is intended to have.

Scenario.   Make up a scene that will grab your audience's attention:

> Imagine—you can land the opportunity of a lifetime! The job you've always dreamed about, with a very prestigious company. The money's a lot more than you're making now. And you've been selected as one of the final candidates. All you have to do is make a presentation to the company's board of directors relating why you're the person best suited for the job. You step up to the head of the conference table, look out at their faces, and...?

   A scenario is a a "word picture" that creates a scene in the mind of the audience. Like a rhetorical question, it entices the audience to partici-pate in your presentation right from the start. Although this example asks the audience to imagine, it's a scene that could actually take place, so people will go along with it. (In fact, I've used this scenario when I've made presentations on presentation skills. I was recently reminded that life imitates art when a friend approached me for help in developing a presentation for this very situation.)

Anecdote.   Sometimes an anecdote is a good way of opening.

> Since I was in the big Alaskan quake in 1964, I am not at all partial to earthquakes. I mention this because it relates to my first experi-ence giving a presentation. I was literally all shook up!
>   I'd been asked to speak to a group of officers at a military base. I did all the right things: knew my subject, prepared beforehand, and arrived early enough to check out the facilities. Everyone filed into a basement conference room where we were meeting. They took their seats, and I stepped to the head of the room. About two minutes into my presentation, there was suddenly a terrible rumbling overhead. The walls shook and the ceiling lights blinked. My heart leaped and I frantically bolted down the aisle for the nearest door! I was

stopped by a gentleman who explained that every hour on the hour, soldiers changed classrooms located on the floor above. The rumbling was caused by two hundred troops marching down the halls in heavy-duty army boots! Needless to say, I wrapped up my presentation before the next changing of the guard!

Are you one of those who finds presenting an "earthshaking" experience?

An anecdote briefly describes an incident that's interesting, amusing, or biographical. The most attention-getting anecdotes are all three. They're most effective when communicated with facial expressions, gestures, and intonations that add interest and amusement, and thus draw in the audience. (Of course, the same thing can be said of your whole presentation.) They also have appeal when they're self-disclosing. Audiences respond more affirmatively to presenters who relate on a human level. Showing something of yourself is a way of doing that. (More on relational skills in Chapter 3.)

Combos.   The most effective opener may be one that uses a combination of types. For example, consider the effect of a declarative statement in combination with a rhetorical question: "Training is a multibillion-dollar industry in this country, and it's a market that's growing every day. What can you do to capture more opportunities in that market?"

Or the authoritative quotation in combination with a question: "According to T. Boone Pickens, 'Leadership is the quality that transforms good intentions into positive action.' How can you demonstrate your ability to transform intentions into positive action?"

On Jokes

Never start a presentation with a joke, especially in a business or professional setting. I suspect the practice started during the days of vaudeville comics and has continued by imitation ever since. It's a practice that should be banned.

Most of us lack the comedic timing to deliver a joke really well. And even for those speakers who can, the joke is all too often one the audience has heard before; or worse, it has no relevance to the subject at hand. Speakers who persist in starting with a few jokes all seem to share the same source: a book entitled *1001 Jokes to Make Audiences Laugh*. Having heard the same ones numerous times before, people don't find them funny anymore. If the audience laughs, it's often out of a sense of courtesy to the speaker, not because the joke is a real attention-getter.

Unless you're delivering a stand-up routine on a Bob Hope special or making a guest appearance at The Improv comedy theater, never start with a joke! Your purpose as a presenter is to persuade by having impact. And bad jokes, or good jokes badly told, can have the opposite effect.

The Best Opener

Given the different types of openers you can use, what's the best way to invite your audience in? There is no one best way. The best opener is one that satisfies your answers to these questions:

- What's most relevant to your subject and to the audience?
- What's most appropriate to the setting?
- What best suits your own personal style, so you can begin comfortably and naturally?

Just remember, the opener to a presentation is like the first paragraph of a book. It's the "hook" intended to capture people's attention. You want an opener that will get the audience sufficiently interested so that they'll stay tuned to hear more.

Introducing You

When I present training in presentation skills, the question that comes up at this point is, "When do I introduce myself?"

If you've been previously introduced, you don't. If you're presenting in a setting where a master of ceremonies makes the introductions, just be sure they have the information they need to introduce you as you wish. Provide the emcee with a single sheet of paper that indicates the title of your presentation and includes a brief biographical sketch. To establish your credibility, your bio should highlight the main points of your background that are related to the topic of your presentation. If your name is other than Smith or Jones, be sure the emcee knows how to pronounce it correctly. It will save you, and them, possible embarrassment.

Once you've been introduced and you step to the platform, open and get on with your presentation. No further commentary about yourself is necessary. If your presentation is poor, no amount of credentials or background will salvage it. If it's good, it will speak for itself.

If you're not introduced by a master of ceremonies or you're not known to the group to which you're presenting, then of course you'd introduce yourself. Do so after the opener and before you state the objective.

Caution: Be brief. If you (or an emcee) take up a lot of time talking about you, it will reduce the impact of your opener and you'll risk losing people's attention. (You'll also risk being perceived as egocentric, which won't endear you to people.)

Think of your self-introduction as an addendum to the opener. It should not be the opener itself. We've all heard presenters begin like this: "Good morning, my name is Jan Doe. I want to thank you for the time to speak with you today." That kind of opening is a major bore. It's been said a million times before. There's nothing attention-getting, meaningful, or memorable about it.

Try this type of approach instead:

> (Opener) Training is a multibillion-dollar industry in this country. And it's a market that's growing rapidly every day. For the individual who presents skillfully, that means a lot of opportunity. (Self-introduction) Good morning, my name is Jan Doe. (A bit of background) As director of corporate training for XYZ Company, I see people present all the time. (Objective) This morning, you'll discover how to become a more skillful presenter so you can take advantage of the opportunities.

Prepare the Closing "To Do"

One measure of your success as a presenter is how well your message effects a desired response. Bringing about the response you want is likely to entail effecting a change: a change in the way people think, a change in the way they behave, a change in the way they've been doing business so that they do business with you.

People aren't usually moved to change by just hearing. We change by doing. So, the last thing you want to leave people with is something specific to do. The last step in preparing your presentation is to develop this closing "to do."

Types of "To Dos"

Present what you want the audience to do after the summary, and state it in one of three ways. Give them a reminder, an application of the information, or request their approval. Each option echoes a type of objective.

Reminder. "Remember: Your presentation will be more persuasive when you customize the approach to your customers." In reminding the audience of a significant principle, you echo the objective: to understand.

Application. "Take a moment to write down three techniques you'll use next time you present." When you present an application of the information, you echo the objective: to be able to.

Approval. "The presentation you've heard today is available on audiocassette. I encourage you to make it available to the managers in your company who present." When you ask for approval, you echo the objective: to do.

In marketing parlance, the "approval" closing is called "Ask for the order!" Even if you're not delivering a sales presentation, you want people to "buy" your ideas. If you've succeeded in persuading them, their approval will be a natural outcome of your presentation. Wording like "I encourage you" is a courteous and comfortable way to ask the audience to buy. Even nonsellers ought to be able to say something like, "I encourage you to give this your approval."

Reviewing Your Outline

Your audience is more apt to respond affirmatively to the closing "to do" when the points you've made steer them in that direction and provide sufficient reason for them to do it. So, after you've prepared the closing "to do," take a few minutes to review your outline. Ask yourself:

> Will the content of this presentation activate people to do what I'm asking?

If not, rethink your outline. Either the key points, supporting material, or closing "to do" will need to be revised.

Finis

We've gone step-by-step through a model outline for preparing a presentation, beginning with a statement of your objective. By developing material that supports the objective, you persuade the audience to satisfy what you want to achieve. Your concluding "to do" then echoes the objective. Thus an effective presentation comes full circle. Rather than being a fragmented laundry list of data, it's an integrated whole.

Presenters who follow this format enjoy more successful outcomes. It makes it easier for you to prepare and present. It makes it easier for the audience to listen and remember. As you become accustomed to the approach through repeated use, you'll find it becomes automatic. With every additional presentation you make, you will take less and less time to prepare. And if you're ever called on to speak extemporaneously, you won't feel you're on the spot. Instead, you'll quickly fill in a model outline in your mind and be able to speak from it with ease.

Whether you deliver spoken or written presentations, the same principles apply. Next time you're asked to submit a written report or proposal, try the same approaches we've covered in this chapter. (That's a closing "to do.") You'll find it simplifies your efforts and helps you produce a better written product, too.

Your Product

Paul Hawken is a successful entrepreneur, author, and presenter. In response to a question from one of his readers, he shares a secret of his success.[3]

> "The main thing to remember is that you are a service, and that the products you sell are the means for providing that service, which is...knowledge, care and attention."

Whenever you make a presentation, you're a kind of entrepreneur. For as long as you have the floor, you're in business for yourself. And your "customers" are the people in your audience. You are "selling" and you want them to "buy" you and your message. Your "product" is ideas and information. Your "service" is the way you deliver your product.

Your aim in presenting is to give people not only knowledge but care and attention as well. In this chapter, we've focused on ways to approach and structure the knowledge you present. How, then, do you convey care and attention? You do so by the way in which you relate to the people in your audience. That's the subject of Chapter 3.

To Prepare Like a PRO, Remember

- Know your customer and tailor your approach to the audience.
- Prepare in three stages.
  1. Outline your ideas

  2. Develop the narrative
  3. Design supplemental materials

- Outline your presentation in this order.
  1. Your objective
  2. The body (key points, supporting material, transitions)
  3. Introductory preview and closing summary
  4. Attention-getting opener
  5. Activating "to do"

- Deliver your presentation in this order.
  1. Introduction: Opener, Objective, Preview
  2. Body: Key Point 1, Supporting Material, Transition
               Key Point 2, Supporting Material, Transition
               Key Point 3, Supporting Material
  3. Closing: Summary and "To Do"

- Stick to the rule of three: No more than three key points.

References

1. Henry J. Pratt, "Overcoming Stage Fright," *Opportunity,* July 1987, p. 28.
2. T. Boone Pickens, Jr., *Boone,* Houghton Mifflin, Boston, 1987, p. 300.
3. Paul Hawken, *The Next Economy,* Ballantine Books, New York, 1983, p. 195.

3
Relating
to People

When John Naisbitt identified the Information Age as one of this country's megatrends, he coined a term presenters should personify: "high touch." Naisbitt observed: "Whenever new technology is introduced into society, there must be a counterbalancing human response—that is, high touch—or the technology is rejected. The more high tech, the more high touch."[1]

Earlier, we viewed a model that illustrated two aspects of a presentation: the informational and the relational. If you think of the information you're presenting as the high-tech component of your message, then how you relate it to people is the high-touch element, as shown in Figure 3-1.

Informational	Relational
(High-Tech)	(High-Touch)

Figure 3-1. Balancing the Informational and Relational

Keeping these two elements in balance is absolutely critical to your success (if success for a presenter is measured, in part, in terms of audience receptivity). If you don't communicate your message in a high-touch, relational way, people are likely to tune out or reject your presentation altogether.

Information alone doesn't persuade people. If it did, no one would smoke and no one would drink to excess. No one would abuse drugs, no one would dump toxic waste into our water reservoirs, no one would demolish rain forests, no one would—the list goes on and on. Time and again, we're exposed to information substantiating that these are dangerous, sometimes life-threatening behaviors. You would think the sheer weight of the information would be convincing. Obviously, it is not.

In spite of all the evidence to the contrary, "information bound" presenters abound. If you've sat through at least five presentations, chances are you've heard at least one such presenter. They're really easy to spot.

Information-bound presenters are those who rely primarily on facts and figures. They speak to the tops of podiums with their attention focused on note cards. They flip through reams of data and show up with stacks of overheads. They hope to convince you of their knowledge and ideas, yet they depend on reading from a script. Information-bound presenters are those who appear to overlook the most important factor in presenting: the people factor!

A presentation is like a handshake. On one hand, you have informational elements; on the other hand, relational elements. Both must come together when you present if you want to have an impact on people.

This chapter focuses on how to "shake hands" with the people in your audience. Regardless of your subject or the setting, people are basically the same. And they respond best when you relate information that's relevant and meaningful to them and when you do so in a manner that suggests an affirmative relationship with them.

Modes

How you incorporate relational elements depends on the mode of presentation. While there are many different settings in which presentations occur, they can be categorized into one of two basic modes: proactive or interactive.

1. *Proactive mode.* In the proactive mode, the presenter is the protagonist who acts on the audience. The message is delivered by a speaker who takes the more vocal, active role. Presentations in the proactive mode include formal speeches and presenter-dominated seminars.

2. *Interactive mode.* By comparison, in the interactive mode, pre-

senter and audience interact, sharing speaking and listening roles. Information is exchanged. While the presenter may play the more dominant role of group leader, the audience is encouraged to get involved vocally. Participative workshops, classrooms (ideally), and meetings (ideally) are examples of the interactive mode.

While this discussion may seem to be touching on the obvious, it is not. What is not obvious to many presenters is: Relational elements that activate the audience belong in both modes. (Hence the terms *proactive* and *interactive,* with emphasis on *active.*)

In the proactive mode, the audience may appear to be passive. After all, they're just sitting there. But the question is: Are they sitting there attuned to what you're saying, or are they sitting there while mentally elsewhere? The public speaker who delivers a speech to hundreds of people makes a grave mistake if he or she assumes the presentation goes one way. Communicating always involves two parties. And in the most effective communication (of which presenting is one form), the listener is mentally active even if not vocally so.

Every presentation has (or should have) an interactive dimension. If they're listening, an audience reacts to what they see and hear. They communicate their reactions in verbal or nonverbal ways. While audiences don't usually verbalize responses in proactive settings, they respond nonetheless. They nod their heads, smile or frown, or (heaven forbid) wear expressions of bland indifference. Presenters who are sensitive to their audiences adjust to the responses they observe.

This give-and-take of responses is interaction, even in formal settings. If a speaker neglects relational elements that encourage positive interaction, people will eventually stop listening. When audiences no longer listen, presenters lose their power to persuade.

So, the question is not whether a presenter should develop an active relationship with the audience. The question is, rather, how to do so. And the answer is: Relational elements are woven throughout a presentation either implicitly or explicitly. In a proactive mode, interaction is implied. In an interactive mode, it's explicit.

Relational Elements

Whether you're presenting to one person or one thousand, four factors will contribute to how well you relate to and with the audience. They are:

- Expectation
- Recognition
- Participation
- Application

You may recall the point made earlier about the importance of giving customers what they want. These are what your "customers"—your listeners—want. The four factors identify people's relational needs. When you incorporate them throughout your presentation and thus meet these needs, you'll have a satisfied audience.

Expectation

Let your audience know what to expect. People generally don't like surprises and they don't like guesswork. As people begin to shift their minds into gear to listen to you, they want some indication of what's coming. It helps them mentally prepare for what they're about to hear.

It's your job as a presenter to make it easy on your listeners. Don't put them to the test of doing the work for you. They won't. You have to do it for them. Letting the audience know what to expect, at the outset of your presentation, is one way of making it easier for them to listen and understand.

Imagine if this book had no table of contents and no chapter titles. Suppose the start of each chapter failed to provide any clue about the material that was going to be presented. Not only would that make your job of reading more difficult, but chances are you'd feel frustrated or confused. You'd tune out and wouldn't accept this message at all.

By analogy, the people in your audience are your readers. They need clues from you. Giving them clues is the first step in bringing them into your presentation and inviting them into a relationship with you.

In large part, you satisfy people's need to know what to expect when you relate the introductory objective and the preview. However, not all the clues you provide are spoken. Other clues are related through the unspoken signals you send. How are you dressed? What's your facial expression? What's your posture when you step up to the front of the room? How composed do you appear? (More on all that in Chapter 4.)

Whenever I prepare to present, I do both a model-outline check and a mirror check. And I ask myself the question:

> What will people in the audience expect based on what they first see and hear?

The answer I hope to get back is this: They'll expect the key points of my message delivered by a confident and credible professional. What would the answer be for you?

Recognition

Successful marketeers find out what the customer wants. (I know I'm being redundant, but the point is important enough to bear repeating.) Once you know that, you can deliver a product that meets their needs and gives them a sense of satisfaction. The same principle applies to presenters and audiences. Imagine, as a member of the audience, leaving a meeting feeling satisfied. (I've been in a few organizations where that would be a rare experience.) Imagine, as the presenter, having that effect on people.

How can you know what the audience wants? How do you tailor the product, your message, to appeal to your listeners? The answer is deceptively simple. It has nothing to do with subjects or topic titles, or how articulate you are. It has everything to do with people.

One thing you can be sure every person wants is attention. From early childhood on, some people go to bizarre lengths to get someone to pay attention to them. We're far more satisfied (and more easily persuaded) by people who pay attention to us than we are by people who don't.

As a presenter, you demonstrate that you're paying attention to your audience by recognizing them. You deliver your message in such a way that you recognize who you're addressing and what's important to them. Then, you're able to tailor your presentation accordingly.

Know Your Audience.   Recognizing the audience begins with knowing who it is you're dealing with. In Chapter 2, we explored some key characteristics that would give you a snapshot of the audience. Knowing your customer was a precursor to selecting the best approach to your subject.

It's also integral to how both you and your message relate to them. For example, if you were asked to make a presentation on computers, would you be addressing business executives, programmers, or new users? Is your audience most concerned about time-and-cost savings, function and performance, or simplicity of use?

You can appreciate this point if you've ever walked into a retail computer store. An all-too-typical scenario goes something like this. You're accosted by a person who delivers a canned presentation. He speaks computerese: bits and bytes, RAM, ROM, DOS, Unix, megahertz. Unless you speak computerese, the presentation has little meaning. You feel confused, frustrated, and maybe just a little bit annoyed that this person is wasting your valuable time. The presenter isn't paying attention to you, relationally; nor is he paying attention to what you need to hear, informationally. Instead, he focuses on the data he wants to get across. It's a presentation dominated by the speaker's concerns.

Unfortunately, this scenario doesn't occur exclusively in retail stores. It extends into boardrooms, corporate training centers, employee meetings, political platforms, and the like. And it's the surest way to turn off an audience.

Effective presenters, on the other hand, deliver a message that's oriented to the audience. They've done their homework so they understand the predominant factors that characterize the people they're addressing. From that, they determine the key points that will have the greatest impact on their listeners. They recognize and pay attention to what will be most meaningful: not to the speaker, but to the audience.

I don't know how many times I've heard a manager deliver a presentation to a group of employees, only to have the message fall on deaf ears. Why? Because the manager related the message from management's perspective. Conversely, I've heard managers present tough issues and gain favorable responses from employees. How do they do it? They recognize and pay attention to what's important to their listeners.

Address Your Message to the Audience.   Once you know your audience, you'll communicate your message more meaningfully if you address it to them.

Presentations are like letters. Addressed incorrectly, they end up in a dead-letter box. If you want your presentations to be well received, you have to address them to the audience. Not just any audience, but this audience that you're speaking to here and now. There are numerous techniques you can use to do so.

For one, sprinkle your presentations with personal pronouns other than *I*. Avoid phrases like "I want to tell you about." (Generally, people don't want to be told.) Instead, use wording like "you'll discover" or "we'll explore." Addressing the audience with "you" and "your" conveys a sense of relating to your listeners on a more personal level.

When you present to small groups or in interactive settings, you have a further advantage. You can (and should) address people by name. Every small-group presenter should master the skill of memorizing and using people's names. There's nothing that makes people feel quite so special. Using someone's name conveys that you're paying attention on an individualized level.

If you address a group for the first time and you're unacquainted with people's names, have tent cards at each place setting (assuming the group is seated at tables). Make a point of arriving early enough to get to know at least two or three people by name. If the presentation is one that allows for introductions of participants at the beginning, repeating people's names as they introduce themselves will help you remember them.

Direct references are a further means for conveying your message in a more personal, relational way. In other words, refer directly to some characteristic that people in the audience have in common. Depending, of course, on the nature of the audience, phrases like these make direct reference to people being addressed:

"For managers like yourselves..."

"Instructors who use this technique..."

"Most salespeople find..."

You may recall the example in Chapter 2 of the corporate director of training who spoke at a business conference on the subject of employee training. Not knowing his audience, he failed to address his message to them. If he'd given thought to using direct references while preparing his presentation, he might have caught the error of his ways. I can hear him practicing ahead of time, saying, "Owners and managers of local businesses like yourselves..." That one technique alone might have caused him to reflect on the content of his message. He would have realized his message was inappropriate to the audience, and he could have revised his presentation accordingly so that it would have been better received.

In addition to using personal pronouns and direct references, give thought to the material you choose. Terminology, examples, supporting data: it's all vitally important, relationally.

The material you use sends a message within your message. When it's relevant to the people you're addressing, it signifies you're relating to them. Inappropriate terms and material can create the impression that either you don't know who you're addressing or worse, you don't care.

You want to leave people with the feeling that your message is intended just for them.

One incident serves to reinforce this point. A popular author appeared as the guest speaker at two separate luncheons. One day he addressed a women's group, the next day, a men's group. I attended the women's luncheon. In support of one of the points he made, he told two anecdotes. Both were related from a decidedly male point of view. You could almost feel the shudders go through the room. At one point, a woman seated next to me leaned over and whispered, "I don't think I'd want my husband telling me that!" He addressed his message incorrectly, and it dropped in the "dead presentation" box!

While the incident may have been understandable, for a professional presenter it was inexcusable. The effective presenter chooses material, or modifies it, so that it appeals to the audience in attendance.

Whenever you present, ask yourself: "What are the right ways to address this message to the people in this audience? What personal pronouns, direct references, terminology and supporting material will convey that I recognize what's meaningful for them?"

Affirm the Audience.   If you recognize what has meaning for people, then you know it's important they feel affirmed. With few exceptions, most people are more attentive and receptive in environments that make them feel good.

While there are specific techniques you can use to know your audience and to address your message to them, affirming people is another matter. It has more to do with attitude than it does with any techniques you might employ.

I'll admit I don't know how to teach an affirming attitude. Oh, there are techniques you can use, like responding to questions with an affirmative "That's a good question, Mr. Smith." But if, in your heart, you believe the question stinks and you wish Mr. Smith would keep his mouth shut, that attitude will show. Mr. Smith will get the derogatory message—through nonverbal, if not verbal, signals. So, too, will other people in the group.

So, how do you affirm an audience? How do you leave people with the feeling that your presentation was a wonderfully positive experience (even if the subject isn't)? The best way I've found is to develop a "Hallmark" kind of attitude. In other words, "Care enough to give the very best."

The very best you have to give is *you*. I'm all for well-organized speeches and articulate speakers. I enjoy creative audiovisuals as much as anyone. Professional attire, good vocal quality, and skilled platform behavior get my vote any day. But none of these factors compares to the human quality of presenters who give something of themselves.

You give of yourself when you're more conscious of the audience and less conscious about you; when your overriding concern is the value of their experience and not yours. You give of yourself when you relate (appropriately) material that's self-disclosing. You develop a knack for giving of yourself when you present, and present, and present. (That's when presenting is fun!)

Think of a presentation as a present. It's your gift of information and ideas. You give that gift to people in return for the time and attention they're giving you. You can carelessly deliver a shabby box that's taken little time and effort to put together. Or you can carefully choose and arrange the contents, giving thought to what the recipient will respond to. You can present your gift in a plain brown paper wrapper or take care to package it so it has appeal. You can maintain a detached attitude, or you can extend yourself, reach out, and deliver your message in a warm and personal way.

I know of no better way to relate to an audience than by bringing a caring attitude to them. That kind of attitude shows. It shows in your posture, your facial expressions, the tone of your voice. By just about everything you bring to your presentation, you communicate to your listeners: "I recognize your presence and your importance. I care about you." Or, you don't. If you don't recognize people in an affirming way, they're not likely to return an affirmative response.

I've described some presenters who erred on one point of technique or another. It's time for an example of one who didn't err. Or, at least, it didn't matter very much. He was the keynote speaker at a conference. (By this time, you probably think all I do is attend conferences and luncheons!)

Because I teach and coach people in presentation skills, I sometimes feel like a movie critic. It's not intentional; it's just an occupational hazard. Consequently, when this speaker started out, I noticed he didn't state an objective or preview. However, I was soon caught up, as was everyone in the audience, in what he had to say. Or, to put it more accurately, in how he was saying it.

It was obvious he liked what he was doing. He gave the audience the distinct impression he liked them. He was enthused about the points he made and self-disclosing in the examples he used. Although there were about two thousand people present, he talked to the audience as though addressing people one on one. He avoided talking *at* the group. He spoke in a friendly, conversational manner, leaned meaningfully toward the audience at key points, and used all the relational techniques we're covering here. And he smiled, genuinely. He earned a rousing, standing ovation.

If one characteristic more than any other marked this presenter's speech, it was that he paid attention to people. He recognized the audience with all the right techniques and, more important, with a caring attitude.

Pacing.   When it comes to recognizing the audience, seasoned presenters recognize one more critical factor. People have a limited attention span. You'll lose their attention if you drone on endlessly in the same tone of voice, on the same point, standing in the same place for too long a time. So vary the pace of your presentation accordingly.

Pacing a presentation is an aspect many speakers overlook. They present as though the audience will keep listening because of who they are or what they have to say. Nothing could be further from the truth. Few of us ever do any one thing continuously for very long.

People come to your presentation from an environment that's fast-paced and growing faster. Their minds are running in fourth gear, and a host of distractions competes for their attention. As our culture becomes increasingly high tech, we're becoming accustomed to shorter and shorter message increments, and to having control over receiving them.

Computer screens flash and change in nanoseconds with the push of a button. Fax machines and copiers deliver fresh images in less time than it takes to load the paper. And almost everyone nowadays has a television set with a remote control. What do you do if a program's not holding your attention? If you're like most of us, you switch channels. And you switch quickly.

A presentation may be viewed as a television program. If it doesn't capture and sustain people's attention, they'll switch channels and go elsewhere mentally. You can, however, save them the trouble. Switch channels for them. How? By building variations into your presentation that alter the pace from time to time.

Change from one key point to the next. Move to a different spot on the platform. Switch to audiovisuals, then switch back to deliver some points personally. Vary your style of delivery: your tone of voice, gestures and expressions, and the type of supporting material you use. Alternately quicken, then slow, the pace. And (when appropriate) provide a touch of comic relief. In these ways, you provide the variety that helps to sustain people's attention.

Participation

Most people I talk with on the subject of presenting agree that audience participation is important. They concur that it's a good idea to get people involved when they're meeting in smaller groups.

"How small a group?"

"Five or ten."

"How about in a classroom of, say, twenty-five or thirty students?"

"Oh, yes. People learn better when they participate."

"Well, if that's the case, why not have people participate with a group of three hundred or three thousand?"

"That's impossible!" you say? No, it is not. Remember: The distinction between the proactive and interactive modes is not in what you do. It's only in how you do it.

Participation is important. It's one of the best means of relating to an audience and encouraging them to relate back to you. When people take part in an experience, they're far more likely to listen and respond than when they're merely passive objects occupying a chair.

Compare your presentation to a stage play. You may be filling the leading role of presenter, but don't view it as a solo act. You want to invite every person in the audience to play a part. In more formal settings or when you address larger groups, you want the audience to play the part of active, attentive listener. It's not an easy role to fill, since most of us aren't trained to listen actively. So how do you get people to participate?

Ask Questions. In both the proactive and interactive modes, questions are a way of drawing people in. The only difference between the modes is this. In the proactive mode, you ask rhetorical questions to which you don't expect a verbalized answer. In the interactive mode, you ask direct questions and wait for someone to voice a response.

Notice how I qualified the response to a rhetorical question. You don't expect a "verbalized" answer. But whether the answer is verbalized or not, the advantage to posing questions is the ame. Questions entice people to listen and formulate answers—even if only in their minds. As a presenter, if you've got their minds working on your material, you've got the audience's attention.

Timing is critical when you pose questions. In a proactive mode, pose a rhetorical question with the appropriate intonation. Pause meaningfully for a brief moment to give the audience an opportunity to absorb the question and start mentally to form a response. Then present the answer, with confidence.

In an interactive mode, that meaningful pause needs to be substantially longer. Allow sufficient time for someone in the audience to answer a direct question. On the average, that may be as long as twenty to thirty seconds, given the time it takes for people to hear and digest the question, mentally formulate their response, work up the courage to speak, and finally vocalize their answer. Yet watch what happens in many interactive settings. Too many presenters wait five or ten seconds, then rush on and answer the question themselves. It's no wonder audiences are frequently discouraged from actively taking part with presenters who barely give them the chance.

In either case, if you ramble on with your discourse immediately after asking a question, you lose the effect questions are intended to create. Whether rhetorical or direct, questions are posed for the purpose of involving the audience. With no pause, there's no participation.

When you ask questions—whether rhetorical or direct—use predominantly open questions. Open questions elicit a response other than a cursory yes or no. They're the WWWWH questions that begin with *who, what, when, where,* and *how.* (Refrain from asking "why" questions. They can be perceived as testy or threatening.)

Open questions are preferable because they're posed in a more thought-provoking form. And that's exactly what you want to do: provoke the audience to think about your message.

Closed questions, on the other hand, begin with words like *can, are, do, will,* and *have.* They're called "closed" because they "close off" the listener's response. From the standpoint of someone in the audience, if all I have to answer is yes or no, I don't have to pay very close attention. I always have a fifty-fifty chance of being right, and the degree to which I participate is minimal.

Look over the following open and closed questions. Consider how differently you respond to each one.

Open: What are some ways you can encourage people to participate? (pause)

Closed: Can you get people in the audience to participate?

Open: How can you use this idea in your company? (pause)
Closed: Will you use this idea in your company?

Open: What does this information mean to you? (pause)
Closed: Does this information mean anything to you?

Obviously, open questions invite greater participation from the audience, even when they're only rhetorical and the participation is only implied.

Recalls.   Asking the audience to recall something is another technique for implying they are participating.

Invite the audience to take part by reflecting on a previous point in your presentation. For example, "If you'll recall, for a moment, the model outline we used for preparing a presentation..." Your listeners shift their minds into gear, and participate as they mentally recall the point.

Reflecting on familiar events is another form of recall. "Remember when the U.S. hockey team won the gold medal at Lake Placid?" "Remember when our astronauts first landed on the moon?" "Remember when a certain governor overstayed his welcome at the podium at the 1988 Democratic National Convention?" "Remember customer reactions to Product X when it was announced?"

Recalling events can be an effective means for stirring people's feelings, for introducing a point, or for developing an analogy—provided it's an event with which the audience is familiar. Participation is implied as people conjure up a mental picture of the occasion and the emotions associated with it.

However, events need to be chosen with care. Not only should they be relevant to your subject, but they need to be relevant to the audience as well. I recall one occasion when I addressed a group of students and said, "Remember when we first landed on the moon?" Now just about everyone my age can tell you exactly where they were and what they were doing at the time. But, no, this particular group didn't remember because most of them hadn't been born yet! The incident reinforced for me the importance of knowing your audience and relating what's meaningful for them. (I attempted to recover from the oversight by quickly switching into a scenario, but it didn't have quite the same effect.)

Scenarios.   A scenario creates a "word picture" or a scene in the mind of your audience. It may be actual or hypothetical; it may be created with anecdotes or verbal illustrations. For example, I might ask you, "Imagine...a senior executive in your organization walks into your next meeting unexpectedly—just as you're about to get up and present your month-end report."

Does a picture start forming in your mind? Do you feel a certain way in response? If so, you're taking part in this presentation.

Scenarios can be an especially effective form of eliciting audience participation in marketing-oriented presentations. Working with a group of architects confirmed how powerful "word pictures" can be. While developing a presentation for a prospective client, we considered ways to persuasively convey the advantages of the firm's design. By describing a scenario that "walked" the client through the building they proposed, the firm convinced the client that their needs were understood. And the client signed the contract. Scenarios, when well done, can create feelings of ownership of the product or service you're trying to sell.

Scenarios can also be a means of persuading people to accept ideas. A public television station periodically broadcasts the Tom Peters presentation, "A Passion for Customers." In it, Mr. Peters opens with a scenario. For those of you who have seen it, you'll recall how he relates an experience with an automotive parts dealer. He describes his attempts to order a part for his new truck. He relates a conversation with the clerk who can't tell him when the part will be in. As he builds this scenario for the audience, he builds their feelings of frustration with poor service.

While he's presenting this scenario, the video cameras periodically scan the audience. People are nodding their heads in agreement as if to say "Yes!" Their expressions confirm, "I can relate to that!" He has effectively drawn them into his presentation.

This example is a particularly good scenario because it does what every presentation piece should. It addresses a very common human experience to which everyone in the audience can relate (so that, by implication, they participate), and it serves to advance the theme of the message.

Mr. Peters follows with facts and figures, statistics that substantiate his point. But this first human interest scenario is what captures people's attention and initiates the relationship between presenter and audience. It's through this "person-to-persons" incident that the audience takes part. When you talk with people who have seen this presentation, this is what they remember—long after they've forgotten the facts and figures.

Does that mean you can dispense with facts and figures? No. You need them to substantiate your points and to add credibility to your position. But data is not as persuasive as drama. Pedantry and percentages have far less impact than the personal interest scenario.

Open questions, recalls, and scenarios can be applied in both proactive and interactive modes. Naturally, in smaller group settings you can create even more opportunities for people to take part—explicitly. Techniques that encourage explicit participation include direct questions, discussions, role playing, workbook exercises, and group problem-solving. They're the tools of the trade for group instructors and facilitators—subjects for another book.

As far as presenting is concerned, remember: Elicit the audience's participation, even if it's only implied. When you do, they'll be involved in an experience that's more meaningful and more memorable for them. Which makes it a whole lot more satisfying for you.

Application

National broadcasts of public figures excepted, Zig Ziglar has probably presented to as many people as anyone else in our time. The people he's addressed number in the tens, maybe hundreds, of thousands. He observes, "We're all tuned in to the same radio station, and its call letters are WIIFM."[2] Translation: "What's In It For Me?"

Most of us are motivated by self-interest. We respond on the basis of what things mean to us. So, the effective presenter never fails to relate a message in terms of how it applies to the audience.

The term *application* has two meanings: (1) how the information can be applied *by* the audience and (2) how it applies *to* them. In other words, what's in it for them.

In Chapter 2 on preparing a presentation, we reviewed an element of structure that satisfies the first meaning: i.e., the closing "to do." The "to do" could also be called the "closing application." When you ask the audience to do something, in effect you're saying, "Here's how my message can be applied by you."

What we want to consider here is how to apply your message *to* people in a way that appeals to their self-interest. Ask yourself:

> What will entice people to pay attention to my message?
>
> What will activate them to carry out my objective?

The answer is *value*. When people perceive value in a product, they're far more likely to buy it. Similarly, when an audience perceives there's value in your ideas and recommendations, they'll be far more likely to listen, accept, and act on them.

This presents a challenge to presenters. We know the value of what we present. If we didn't, we wouldn't take the time or make the effort to get up in front of all those people and try to persuade them to our way of thinking (or the thinking of the organization we represent). As a result, some presenters deliver with blinders on. Knowing the value in what we have to offer, we err if we assume that the audience knows it, too. Always assume they don't—unless you tell them.

Persuasive presenters do what successful sellers do. They mentally crawl into their customer's skins, so to speak. They attempt to view their message from the perspective of the audience, and ask, "What would 'sell' me if I were listening to this from their point of view?"

To determine how to apply your message to people, first identify its value to the audience. Reconsider each key point in light of the question, "What's in this that would benefit my listeners?" Once you've identified audience-related benefit(s), develop appropriate value statements. Statements like these communicate value.

"What this means to you is…"

"As a result, you'll gain…"

"A significant advantage is…"

"Revenues are expected to increase by as much as…"

"You can reduce costs by as much as…"

Use words like *gain, save, potential,* and *increase.* They appeal to people's self-interest.

When I deliver seminars, for example, on the subject of presenting, I sprinkle my presentation with specific value statements like these:

"As a result, you'll save time and effort."

"What this means to you is an opportunity to gain exposure."

"The real advantage lies in the potential to increase your earnings…(pause)…in some cases, substantially."

Value statements should be incorporated throughout your presentation, notably after you've related each key point, and again at the end of your presentation. The more specific you are, the better. Don't leave it up to the audience to infer value based on what you say. They may not make the effort, or they may come to a conclusion different from what you intend.

If more teachers expressed the value of the lessons they presented from the students' perspective, I suspect we'd have fewer school dropouts. If more preachers clarified the value in their Sunday sermons from the congregation's standpoint, I imagine more church-goers would behave differently Monday through Saturday. If more managers expressed the value of company decisions from the point of view of the employee, I suspect more employees would respond favorably. If people who present stated explicitly, "What this means *to you* is…," people in the audience would more readily understand and accept how the message applies to them.

Stating the value of your message means that you have an audience that's more receptive because you've given them reason to listen. A significant advantage is that people will be more motivated to act on what you've said. As a result, your experience as a presenter will be more rewarding: personally, professionally, and financially. Now those are statements of value!

"Person-alize" Your Presentations

When you first begin to present, there's a distance between you and the audience. You're up here. They're out there. And they have no idea what you're going to do. Personalizing your presentation closes the gap that initially exists between you and your listeners. By personalizing, you relate to one another—not as officious presenter and subordinate audience—but as persons engaging in a common experience.

How do you "person-alize" a presentation? How do you encourage an audience to interact with you? In what ways can you relate your message so that your listeners respond as though you were trusted associates or friends?

We've covered a number of techniques that give you a good start. Know your audience so you're prepared with material that pertains specifically to their interests and needs. Recognize them with addresses and affirmations. Elicit their participation (even if they're only involved by implication). And relate what your message means to them in terms of value. The effect of doing all of these things is like engraving an individual's name on a plaque. It personalizes the product.

But the most effective presenters go a step further. They hand-deliver the plaque. It's a gesture that reveals certain personal characteristics about the giver, the presenter. Some of the characteristics that contribute to personalization are covered in more depth in the next chapter. But it's timely to mention two, in particular, here.

The first is that you appear personable: agreeable, pleasant, attractive. That does not mean physically attractive, but rather, that people are attracted to you like a hummingbird to a flower. The audience perceives that you're approachable. They see you as the kind of person they'd like to sit down with and talk to one on one.

I've seen presenters who put on a persona the moment they step up to the front of a room. You can almost hear a little voice going off in their heads, "I have to be a perfect professional now." (I know. It used to go off in my head.) I'd like to silence that little voice with one word of advice: *Relax.* Let down your guard and let people see something of the real you.

That brings us to the second factor in personalizing that works hand-in-hand with the first. Develop a willingness to self-disclose. Disclosing something of yourself sends a signal to the audience that you're operating on a personal level. It implies your involvement with your subject and your commitment to the audience. A self-disclosure can also act as an ice-breaker when delivered with a touch of humor.

Knowing when and what and how much to disclose takes sensitivity and discretion. While revealing certain things about yourself can endear an audience to you, "spilling your guts" is unnecessary, inappropriate, and potentially offensive.

Self-disclosure is really a form of supporting material. You can support a point you're making with a personal anecdote or an example from personal experience. As with every other aspect of presenting, it should be relevant to the audience, the subject, and the setting. (But, of course, by now that goes without saying.)

The effect of personalizing your presentation is like the process of filming. Imagine a cameraman is standing at the back of the audience, filming your presentation. He aims the camera on you and opens with a long-distance, wide-angle shot. You appear small, detached, untouchable. With every relational technique you employ, he adjusts the zoom lens. Your image enlarges until you appear lifelike and in perfect focus. That's how you want to appear to an audience: close up and personal.

An effective presentation contains so much more than just well-organized facts and figures. It consists of building a relationship with people who are giving you the benefit of their time and attention. (You may be able to mandate their time, but you have to earn their attention.)

It's relating your message to the audience in a personalized way that involves them in the occasion. It's keeping in balance high-tech information with high-touch relational elements. That's when presentations have the power to persuade: when you deal with people "person-to-persons."

Next time you have a presentation to make, ask yourself:

> What will I do to *relate* to people more effectively?

When you incorporate the relational techniques presented in this chapter, you'll be wonderfully pleased with the results. And so will your audiences!

To Relate Like a PRO, Remember

- Relate what is relevant: to the audience and to your subject

- Satisfy these four relational needs:

Expectation	State the objective and preview.
Recognition	Know your audience. Address your message to them. Affirm them. Vary the pace of your presentation.
Participation	Ask questions. Use recalls. Relate scenarios.
Application	State how your message applies to the audience in terms of value (from their perspective).

- Person-alize the way you present.

References

1. John Naisbitt, *Megatrends,* Warner Books, New York, 1982, p. 39.
2. Zig Ziglar, *Top Performance,* Fleming H. Revell Company, New Jersey, 1986, p. 222.

4
Optimizing Your Effectiveness

In June of 1987, *Washington Post* columnist Bart Barnes observed of the late, great Fred Astaire:

> He almost always seemed to feel good about himself and enjoy what he was doing. This made his audience enjoy it, too. Hollywood's initial scouting report on him was, "Can't sing...can't act...can dance a little." His voice was thin and reedy, but his presence on the screen more than compensated for that.

Fred Astaire was a real pro! Not about to be put off by the initial report on his talents (or lack thereof), he went on to star in forty films over a period of almost fifty years. The secret of his success? He captivated audiences. Fred Astaire was an optimum performer.

If you were to take a few minutes right now and write a review of how you present, how would it read? Would you describe yourself as an "optimum performer"? In my experience working with business clients and students, most answer "No." If that's true for you, your answer could become a resounding "Yes!"

In the preceding chapters, we've covered some techniques for preparing a presentation and determining how best to relate it to your audience. By analogy, these steps parallel what a Fred Astaire would have done in rehearsals. They're part of the process of getting ready before you actually take to the stage.

Once you're on stage before an audience, the quality of your performance depends on the quality of your delivery. Skillful delivery

Figure 4-1. Delivery

optimizes the effect of a presentation and elevates it from just okay to outstanding!

Delivery

Delivery refers to the methods by which you communicate the "what" you have to say to the "who." You deliver your message to people through three channels: verbal, vocal, and visual (as illustrated in Figure 4-1).

Most of the time and effort you spent preparing your presentation was probably expended on words. Choosing the right words. Writing words. Practicing the words you're going to say. So "what" you're going to deliver is a message. A message of what? Of words. Right? Wrong! Or at least, not altogether right.

In studies of face-to-face communication, Dr. Albert Mehrabian found that words are far less crucial to a message than most people would expect. His findings revealed that the impact of the three channels of delivery varies considerably (Figure 4-2). Visual cues (what's seen) accounted for more than half of the impact on people. More than a third came from vocal signals (sounds and tones). Less than a tenth was the result of words (the verbal channel).[1]

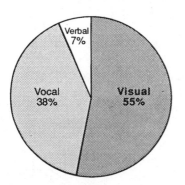

Figure 4-2. Relative Impacts of Channels of Delivery

That's not to say words aren't important. They are. Presenting is a vehicle for persuasion. And a presenter who demonstrates a good command of the language will more favorably influence an audience than one who doesn't. Words are packed with meanings beyond their dictionary definitions. But words alone don't make a presentation.

What is most significant about Mehrabian's findings is not the discovery that words have relatively nominal impact. It's that the visual and vocal channels have so much! Together, they account for more than ninety percent of the impact of a presentation. And yet, even given these findings, how many times have you heard presenters who relied predominantly on words? (This is another reminder that we're not persuaded so much by facts as we are by feelings.)

How do you feel watching a Spielberg movie? Or a televised special? You are moved, not so much by the script as by sights and sounds. Television commercials offer confirmation. Major advertisers impress their products upon people through strong visual images and vocal signals. Through these, viewers and listeners perceive the product as satisfying something they want. We feel the excitement of a blazing red sports car roaring around the curves of a mountain road. We warm to the friendship expressed on the smiling faces of people seated around a table as glasses clink and the wine is poured. We feel the romance of walking hand in hand through a meadow, melodious music filling the background. Even if the words were eliminated, we would still receive the essence of the messages.

Presenters can learn a lesson from advertisers about the power of perceptions and about influencing perceptions through vocal and visual cues. The people in our audiences are viewers as well as listeners. And they are accustomed to an endless array of audiovisual media: television, videotapes, movies, computers, and multiscreen presentation aids. As the messages and media to which people are exposed become increasingly sophisticated, the need becomes ever greater for presenters to master skillful, dynamic delivery. Audiences are disappointed with a presenter who just talks. They look for, in both presenter and presentation, a "product" that satisfies what they want (and what they are coming to expect).

We've considered how organizing information in an easy-to-follow manner satisfies—in part. Knowing your audience and relating to them in meaningful terms satisfies—in part. In this chapter we consider delivery factors that satisfy the audience further and thus optimize your effectiveness.

As we proceed, bear in mind that as the presenter, you're the most important factor. All the verbal, vocal, and visual channels through which a presentation is delivered begin and end with you. In effect, you are your own best (or worst) audiovisual.

Imagine that you're seated in the audience. You might be one among a small group attending an office meeting; one of a hundred associates attending a service club luncheon; or one of a thousand seated at a business convention. Regardless of the setting, what's the first thing that happens after a presenter is introduced? The speaker steps up to begin the presentation. In the thirty to sixty seconds it takes the presenter to get to the head of the room, you're looking and already forming an impression based solely on what you see.

Then, the speaker's voice comes across the room. How would you describe the sound? Strong or shaky? Confident or coy? Pleasant or grating? How does it affect you as a member of the audience? You continue to form an impression based secondarily on the voice you hear. Before the presenter has even approached the "meat" of the presentation, people in the audience have formed impressions!

Audiences see you *before* they hear you (as well as while they hear you). What you deliver visually influences how receptive the audience is to what you say.

Audiences hear, not just words, but the vocal characteristics in which your words are clothed. As a presenter, what you deliver vocally influences what the audience perceives you're saying.

It's no accident that accomplished presenters raise and lower their voices at certain times. It's no accident that successful business professionals favor dark conservatively tailored suits. It's no accident that a speaker leans forward one moment and then steps back the next. These aren't accidental occurrences. They're done purposefully to elicit certain responses.

In a word, what you deliver to an audience is based on what and how you *project*. By analogy, movie projectors in theaters cast images and transmit sounds. A picture is projected on the screen; a sound track accompanies it. People respond to what's projected emotionally as well as rationally (and often more emotionally than rationally). The audience is pleased or displeased. They feel good or they feel bad. They want more or they just want to get up and go home.

In some respects, presentations are like movie projections. The same attention to detail that goes into directing a movie ought to go into delivering a presentation. There is, however, one significant difference. Presenters don't get chances to do retakes. All the more reason for being well prepared before you present.

What details should you attend to in order to deliver an optimum presentation? They're the details of visual, vocal, and verbal delivery, and the personal style that you project. With each, bear in mind four criteria for effective delivery. What you project should (1) fit the setting, (2) support your message, (3) awaken the audience, and (4) be delivered in moderation.

Fitting the Setting

Presentation settings can generally be described as formal or informal (with variations between both extremes). Certain behaviors are appropriate in one setting but not suited to another. For example, standing behind a podium may be the norm in a formal situation. Maintaining the same position in an informal setting will create the perception of a barrier.

Supporting the Message

Remember the rule of thumb: If it doesn't support the objective, don't do it. Likewise, if what you project doesn't support your message, don't do it. Intonations, gestures, audiovisual media, and other delivery techniques have no value in and of themselves. They are simply tools for the purpose of adding expression to the content. Doing something solely for dramatic effect won't contribute to your effectiveness. If anything, it's likely to distract the audience, and it may confuse your meaning. So whatever you do in the way of enhancing delivery, make sure it supports the message.

Awakening the Audience

One of the criteria of an effective presentation is that it gets and keeps the audience's attention. The longer your presentation, the more critical this becomes, because people have short attention spans. Consequently, you want to project in a manner that keeps the audience alert. Depending on the nature of the setting and the subject, your delivery may be lively one day, forceful the next, or varied during the same presentation. However you deliver a presentation, by all means avoid being dull.

Projecting in Moderation

There's truth to the old familiar adage, "Everything in moderation." Anything done to extremes can be distracting. More is not necessarily better. Moderation is achieved by keeping in balance the criteria described above and refraining from excesses, melodrama, or gimmicks.

These criteria serve to guide a presenter's behaviors. I might, for example, suggest that a certain movement accentuates meaning. But if it's not appropriate to the setting in which you present or doesn't support your message, then it's not something you should do. So as we discuss projection and delivery skills, bear in mind that they are not used in a vacuum. Visual, vocal, and verbal techniques are applied (and adapted) in relation to the whole presentation: the content of your message, the setting, the audience—and your own personal style.

What You Project Visually

In a local election, early polls showed one candidate had a substantial lead. In the final three weeks before the election, campaign ads appeared on television featuring the candidate addressing the community. He lost the election. From what I observed, it was not what he said that lost him votes. It was, interestingly, a very subtle visual signal he projected.

If you watch television, you'll spot the same thing in some public speakers. It's a movement of the head that undermines the message. The speaker says, "I firmly believe we can achieve our goals." While these affirmative words are being spoken, the head is shaking back and forth in a movement we commonly perceive to signal no. The audience receives a mixed message. Since the visual impact is stronger than the verbal impact, the message they perceive from the speaker is, "I don't believe we can achieve our goals." Or worse, "I'm lying."

If you're skeptical about how powerful such visual signals are, try this little test. Speak to someone about an issue on which you want to gain their agreement. Say something like, "I think that's a good idea. What do you think?" As you're speaking, ever-so-subtly nod your head up and down, signifying "yes." Chances are she'll mirror your behavior. She'll start nodding her head up and down, too.

The visual channel of delivery is more powerful than most people realize. And it's made up of many different factors. Presenters, in particular, should be acutely aware of what they're projecting through various vehicles of visual communication: head movements and facial expressions, platform behavior, and by the presence they project overall.

Head Movement, Facial Expressions, and Eye Contact

We've considered an example of how head movement can reinforce or detract from a presentation. We transmit an amazing number of messages (often subconsciously) through telling head movements and facial expressions, and what we say with our eyes.

In one situation I coached a manager who, when asked questions from the audience, glanced up at the ceiling momentarily while she gathered her thoughts. It was a habitual response of which she wasn't even aware. But it had the unfortunate effect of signaling a kind of vacuous response to the question, as though the presenter had mentally drifted off. I suggested she glance instead toward the foot of the first row of chairs (not down, but out at about a forty-five degree angle), adding a thoughtful expression of interest or concern. That one slight adjustment made all the difference in the world.

What's your response when someone looks down or away, and avoids making eye contact with you? What do you perceive from someone who cocks his head to one side and slightly furrows his brows? How do you feel when someone holds up her head, meets your glance, and smiles with genuine warmth?

Be conscious of your head movements when you present. A nodding motion up and down communicates affirmation. A shaking motion side to side communicates denial. Tilting your head can suggest curiosity or uncertainty, depending on the facial expression that accompanies it. Holding your head up communicates confidence, especially when coupled with a facial expression of composure.

When you're in front of a group as the presenter, you can tell how the audience is responding. You read their reactions from the expressions on their faces. Similarly, people in your audience derive meaning from you on the basis of your facial expressions.

Here, again, you want to be aware of the visual signals you're sending. Is your expression intense or relaxed? serious or smiling? forceful or fearful? One is not necessarily better than the other. They're different. And different facial expressions, like head movements, support or deny the meanings you intend to deliver.

To impress this point on novice presenters, I ask them to view scenes from old movies. You can do this yourself if you ever stay up and watch the late show on television. In the 1930s and 1940s, film makers lacked the special effects that are available to directors today. Much more had to be communicated facially. When you watch some of these old movies, turn off the sound. Observe the expressions on people's faces. You'll become more sensitized to the power to communicate that's in your own face.

Many people, especially those new to presenting, appear to put on a mask when they present. One moment, they're having a cup of coffee and enjoying a friendly chat. They're conversing expressively, and their faces fairly shine. Ten minutes later, the meeting reconvenes. It's their turn on the agenda. They step up to the head of the room to present, and put on a serious (!) expression. It's either a response to what they perceive to be appropriate to the role of presenter, or it's intended to mask their anxiety over speaking in public.

Whichever the case may be, if I see the mask go on when I coach presenters, I stop their presentations. I ask them to sit down and just talk to me. "Tell me what you want to say...just talk to me." A wonderful transformation occurs. Their faces are enlivened and expressive. You see reflected in them genuine concern or enthusiasm. The meaning they want to relate to an audience is expressed when they present one on one.

The moral of the story is this: If you sense that facial expressions are not your strong suit, present as though you were just talking to someone, one on one. Even when you address an audience of one hundred or one thousand, view that audience as one—one composite person who will see reflected in your face more meaning than they'll hear from mere words.

Of all the features on your face, none is more expressive than your eyes. If you've ever taken a course in public speaking or read a book about presentation skills, you've heard repeatedly about the importance of eye contact. It is important because it sends a visual signal to your viewers that you're connecting with them. It's a technique that distinguishes relational presenters from nonrelational, information-bound speakers.

To make and maintain eye contact is more than just looking at people. How you look at an audience is far more important than the fact that you look at them. It's been said the eyes are the mirror of the soul. If in your soul you dislike what you're doing, that will show through your eyes—no matter how many eyes in the audience you contact. On the other hand, if you're enthused about your subject and you care about your audience, your eyes will reflect your enthusiasm and caring. And the audience will respond in kind.

People who need to present to large groups raise the question, "How do I make eye contact with the whole audience?" You don't. You create the impression that you're relating to everyone in the group with a technique that sweeps the audience.

Picture the room like the face of a clock. As you present, make a point of addressing the major points on the clock: 12, 3, 6, and 9. Avoid repeatedly following a clockwise pattern, or the pattern will become obvious and distracting. Instead, vary the directions in which you move your eyes around the face of the room. Address points 12, 3, 6, and 9; then 6, 12, 9, and 3, and so on.

After a while, you will not be aware of the points on the clock. As you present more and more, you'll develop the habit of connecting with the whole audience, easily and naturally. They'll perceive you're making focused eye contact with the whole group.

Maintaining connection with an audience through eye contact takes some finesse when you need to refer to notes or audiovisuals. We'll address the subject of audiovisual media in the next chapter. As to referring to notes: People who deliver optimum presentations know their material intimately. As a result, they're not dependent on their notes and they are free to relate better to the audience.

I am not suggesting you should never refer to notes. Your presentation may be lengthy or complex. It may contain a critical point you don't want to overlook. If you're citing facts and figures, you want to be sure you get them right. Those are all occasions when notes come in handy.

How do you handle notes and still maintain meaningful eye contact? The same way television news anchors do. Watch the way they operate. They keep their heads up and maintain eye contact with their viewers. Occasionally, they drop their eyes to glance quickly at their notes, but they just as quickly reestablish eye contact. (I know. They have the benefit of referring to teleprompters. But they also have the burden of delivering new "presentations" two or three times a day, without the time to prepare beforehand that you should have when you present.)

Notice the way newscasters handle note sheets: very inconspicuously. They don't lift the papers up (a visual distraction) or ruffle them (an auditory one). Instead, they continue to speak and maintain eye contact while they quietly slip the top sheet to the side and under the others. Very subtle. You want to demonstrate that same kind of subtlety when you present so that the audience's attention is on you and on your message—not on note cards, papers, or other distractions.

If you want the audience's attention on you, your attention should be on them. Be sufficiently conversant with your subject that you don't have to rely on notes continuously throughout your presentation. When your head is buried in scripts and note cards, you can't sustain eye contact with the audience. You won't express much facially. And you won't gain the benefit of skilled platform behavior.

Platform Behavior

Like most presenters, I wasn't surprised when I read a newspaper article that reported the following finding: People who present expend as much energy in four hours as the average office worker does in a full day. Anyone who's been up on their feet, giving to audiences, knows that is true. It's especially true of optimum presenters who "perform" a message as much as they present it.

There are probably thousands of people in this country who dance. But there was only one who performed like Fred Astaire. Just about anyone can tap their toes and kick up their heels. But only real pros transform those movements into meaning and deliver them with panache—much to the delight of audiences.

Similarly, there are thousands (maybe hundreds of thousands) of people in this country who present. But there are few who do so optimally. Just about anyone can speak. But only the real pros transform pieces of information into movements that communicate meaning. They're the ones who deliver a presentation with panache—much to the delight of audiences.

The movements a presenter makes are collectively termed "platform behavior." When I hear the term, I'm reminded of Greg Louganis, the world's greatest Olympic gold medal diving champion to date. Picture Greg Louganis stepping onto a diving platform. He's composed. His posture and movements when he springs off the platform combine to deliver a winning "presentation."

Picture yourself when you're on the "platform": the front of a conference room, a small classroom, or an auditorium stage. Are you ready to "dive" into your presentation? You can remain standing stiffly at one point on the floor, locked rigidly in place. You may position yourself behind a protective podium or next to a projector. Or, you can embellish your message with gestures and movements and deliver a more winning presentation.

Appropriate gestures and movements add meaning to a message. A mime's performance is a classic example. The whole presentation is delivered through skillfully expressed movements. Communication occurs without a word being spoken.

For a presenter, gestures add physical expression to the spoken word. They illustrate or reinforce the points you're making. They give emphasis and energy to a presentation. In that way, they also serve to sustain the audience's attention.

Gestures and movements also serve to minimize barriers that may exist between a presenter and the audience. One such barrier is a solid wood podium. It's like a wall between you and the people you're addressing. Unfortunately, some settings mandate that you stand at a podium, but they don't mandate that you stand there rigid. Leaning toward the audience at appropriate points and periodically moving to one side or the other helps create the impression that you're at ease and connecting with people. (You may notice that, more and more, transparent acrylic podiums are being used.)

If you're free to move around the platform, step lively in order to keep the audience alert. Walk purposefully, maintaining eye contact as you move. Move forward toward the audience on occasion, and then back to the podium or table to check your notes. And vary the path you take. On one point, you may speak from the right side of the platform; on the next you may present from center stage.

However you move, refrain from pacing back and forth, back and forth, in the same direction and always at the same speed. You don't want people thinking your presentation is like watching a tennis match. You don't want to look like a caged lion waiting for someone to toss you a piece of meat. And you don't want the audience lulled or distracted by a repetitive movement.

When you're on the platform presenting, stay up on your feet. In some settings, like seminars and classrooms, I've seen speakers use a presenter's stool. In my experience, the only place a presenter's stool belongs is in the corner where it won't get in the way. Sitting inhibits gestures and movement. It also diminishes energy. When we sit, we tend to slump. When we slump, we don't breathe deeply; our energy supply drops. If you're going to deliver a powerful presentation, you need all the energy you can muster! The energy you exhibit is transmitted to the audience and helps to keep their attention level up.

Developing effective platform behaviors can take practice. It's one of the reasons to present every chance you get. When it comes to presenting, practice can make perfect—practice, and the insights you can gain from observing accomplished presenters.

Whenever you're seated in an audience, pay particular attention to what presenters do. What do you respond most favorably to? Notice the gestures and movements that enhance the message. Those are the things you want to project to your audience when you're on the presenter's side of the platform. Emulate behaviors that appeal to you. Notice, too, those that are distracting. They're the behaviors you want to avoid.

The more practiced and relaxed you become as a presenter, the more naturally you'll gesture and move in ways that complement your spoken words and the overall effect you want to create. If you haven't reached that comfort level yet, concentrate on just one item at a time. During your next presentation, work on gestures. During the next, add head and body movements. During the next, practice moving around the platform in relation to the audience, notes, and audiovisuals. With each subsequent presentation you'll add to your repertoire of platform skills. In time you'll find you're "working the room" with proficiency and ease.

Presence

The visual channel of delivery is so powerful that it accounts for more than half of the impact a presenter has on people! The way an audience views a speaker is every bit as critical as what they hear. There's probably no visual aid that has more influence on people than the presence a presenter projects.

The review of Fred Astaire that opened this chapter concluded with this observation: "His voice was thin and reedy, but his presence on the screen more than compensated for that." What he may have lacked (initially) in talent, he made up for with a pleasing and powerful presence. It's an asset for anyone who presents.

Presence encompasses a number of factors. *Presence* is defined as "something present of a visible or concrete nature; the bearing, carriage, or air of a person; a quality of poise and effectiveness that enables a performer to achieve a close relationship with his audience." Presence is what people project when they've mastered the full gamut of presentation and delivery skills.

How do you establish a presence? Start with your attire. It's the something that's most visible and concrete. How you first appear when you begin to present is the first consideration in establishing your "presence."

The preferred attire for presenters satisfies two requirements. It should contribute to the perception you want to create. And it shouldn't distract from your message. After you deliver a presentation, you want people thinking and talking about what you said—not about how you looked or what you wore. You want the audience aware of your presence; but you don't want your presence overwhelming your presentation.

A conversation I had with an acquaintance illustrates this point. I joined her and her boss for lunch one day to discuss staff development programs for their firm. As she and I walked out together afterward, I complimented her on her hair. She laughed. "Well," she said, "I could use some of that presentation training myself. Whenever I present, people come up afterward and the only thing they comment on is my hair!" She did have beautiful hair. She just had too much of it—at least for a person presenting serious subjects in business and professional settings.

On another occasion, I was seated next to an acquaintance during a conference. A few minutes into a speaker's presentation, my friend leaned over and remarked: "Good grief, he must make a lot of money! Just look at that ring he's wearing!" Every time the speaker gestured, the spotlight bounced sparkles of light off the large diamond in his ring.

It doesn't take much to distract people. Here you've poured your heart and soul into getting ready for an important presentation, and people in the audience walk away commenting on your tie clip or your earrings! If you don't want that happening to you, avoid potentially distracting attire and accessories.

Ladies: Avoid fingernails that are too long or painted too brightly; hair styles that are too long or too fluffed up; jewelry that's too dangly and obvious; clothing that's faddish or too bright.

Gentlemen: Avoid ties and shirts that are too bold or bright; rings or tie clips that are too large or glittery; hair that's too long or unkempt; coats and slacks that are mismatched or appear in need of a good pressing.

Overall, avoid anything in the way of attire (including personal grooming and accessories) that may hinder or dominate your presentation. A flashy, faddish appearance may be fine for an entertainer, but it diminishes the presence of a presenter. The successful presenter, like the successful business person, dresses for success. And in a business setting, there's still nothing that beats the muted, conservatively tailored suit.

Your attire makes a strong visual statement right from the outset of your presentation, and it can enhance or detract from your credibility. You can step before a group with all your credentials intact: degrees, experience, testimonials. But if your attire doesn't conform to your credentials, your credentials will suffer. (Remember? Perception is more powerful than fact.) If the audience doesn't perceive you to be credible, why would they be persuaded to accept your message?

Presence also refers to "the bearing, carriage, or air of a person." Good posture and a confident demeanor contribute to how you're perceived. People who slouch or project uncertainty will have a doubly difficult task commanding the audience's attention. If you stand or walk or move in ways that convey "I'm not sure about this," the audience will respond in kind. "If you don't have confidence in what you're doing, why should we?"

The real key to establishing a presence that appeals to an audience lies in striking the right balance. You do want to avoid slouching. Visually, it suggests you're uncertain or indifferent. You don't want to stand so rigid and upright that you give the impression of being nervous or uptight. You do want to project competence and self-assurance. You don't want to appear superior or self-important.

In effect, presence is a matter of being present with the audience in the same manner in which you want them present with you. You want them to be alert, attentive, and confident in you and genuinely interested in the subject. When that's what you want from your listeners, that's what you have to project.

What You Project Vocally

A very simple exercise illustrates the impact of vocal signals. Ask half a dozen people to say the single-syllable word *oh*. If the people you ask are at all expressive, you'll hear a range of responses like, "Oh?" "*oh!*" "oooohh," and "Ooh#@!$%." The seemingly insignificant *oh* can take on significant meaning, depending on the vocal signal that accompanies it. That's true of how you deliver words throughout your presentation.

Vocal effectiveness is influenced by four factors: quality, intonation, pauses, and fillers.

Quality

Vocal quality includes the pitch, volume, rate, and tone of your voice. Simply stated: Is your voice high-pitched or low-pitched? Do you speak loudly or softly? quickly or slowly? Is the tone of your voice pleasant, resonant, shrill, or grating? The optimum vocal quality is midrange. The best speakers deliver words in a moderate pitch, at a moderate volume and rate of speech, in well-modulated tones (with some variations, of course, to keep it interesting).

Intonation

Raising, lowering, and altering the tone of your voice is an especially important vocal attribute (as our little exercise with *oh* demonstrated). Nothing will put an audience to sleep faster than a monotone, and it's tough to be persuasive when people are dropping off to sleep. Appropriate intonation adds interest and variety, which sustains the audience's attention. More important, appropriate intonation adds meaning to your message, which makes it more memorable for your listeners.

In addition to expressing meaning, intonation can add emphasis. But emphasizing a point doesn't necessitate raising your voice. I've heard presenters practically shout at the audience to impress a point upon their listeners as though they were deaf. Instead of beating the podium with their fist, they beat the air with their words, like a used car dealer making a pitch on a television commercial. Not only can this "shouting" be offensive, but it doesn't work nearly as well as the reverse technique. Next time you want an audience really to listen to you, lower your voice and speak more slowly and deliberately.

Effective intonation is appropriate intonation. Avoid intoning just for the sake of it. Doing so can detract from your message, as I discovered during a training session I attended. A few minutes into one presenter's segment, I found myself struggling to listen for the meaning. Then it struck me why that was so. The speaker raised the tone of her voice for, say, ten phrases; then lowered her voice for the next ten; then raised her voice for ten phrases, and so on. The pattern was so predictable it had the effect of a vocal seesaw. As such, it was almost as sleep inducing as a monotone.

Appropriate intonation matches the tone of voice with the meaning you intend to invest in a word or phrase. After all, that's the primary function of intonation: more clearly or emphatically to express or magnify meaning. Intonation to sustain the audience's attention is only a secondary result. When you achieve the first, you automatically accomplish the second.

Pauses

Meaningful intonation is one technique that enhances vocal delivery. So, too, is sometimes saying nothing at all.

Presenters who feel compelled to speak nonstop do themselves, and their audiences, a disservice. They put themselves under tremendous pressure, which usually results in their speaking too loudly or too fast. They never step away from the podium for fear of missing a beat. And just to be sure there's nary a moment of silence, they fill in all the blanks with "ers" and "ums" and "ahs." Disastrous!

Relax a bit and give yourself a break. It's a break the audience may appreciate, too. All the while you're speaking, they're at work listening, and they don't know what's coming next (which makes their job tougher). A pause gives them a chance to catch up. A moment of silence allows them mentally to digest what they've heard. And you can intentionally pause to let a point sink in.

The best times to insert intentional pauses are after rhetorical questions and between key points. Another time when pausing comes in handy is if you've mentally lost your place and need to check your notes. In this case, the pause may not have been what you really intended, but the audience won't notice the difference if you handle it well.

Suppose you've moved away from the podium and you're delivering a point close to the audience. You find you need to return to the podium to check your notes. Deliver what I call a "preface to the pause." (It acts as a bridge to get you over the hump.)

Here's how it goes. You draw a mental blank and need to pause. While maintaining eye contact with the audience (as you step your way back to your notes), state your preface to the pause. Depending on the nature of your message and where you stop, these kinds of phrases do the trick: "In addition, we want to consider this factor." "Another noteworthy point…," or "We've been talking about X. What follows…?" (as though you're posing a rhetorical question). In the worst possible case, you can always say, with humor and a smile, "Now, where were we…?" Then follows the pause while you check your notes and collect your thoughts; and then you're ready to go on.

Fillers

Pauses, whether they're intentional or not, are much more preferable than fillers. *Fillers* are the words and phrases a presenter uses to fill up every silence. They're the little "ers," "uhs," "okays," and "ums" that drive an audience to distraction. Vocally, they interrupt the flow of a message and signal uncertainty on the part of the presenter. In fact, you may not feel uncertain, but the audience may perceive you to be.

Using fillers is often an unconscious habit. You can detect if your presentations are plagued by them by tape-recording yourself when you present. In fact, as convenient and inexpensive as tape recording is, it's a terrific tool for evaluating how you vocalize overall. Your dearest friend and strongest advocate can tell you all day long, "You say 'uh' too often." If you're like most of us, you won't welcome the criticism. And if you're not aware you're doing it, you may not really believe it. By listening to a tape recording of your presentation, you'll hear yourself and be more likely to correct the problem. Since what you project vocally accounts for more than a third of the impact you have when you present, it is worth a little inexpensive self-evaluation.

What You Project Verbally

Compared to visual and vocal channels, Dr. Mehrabian's findings indicate that words are relatively unimportant in the overall scheme of face-to-face communication. Nonetheless, the words you use can have a greater or lesser effect. To optimize your presentations, you want to verbalize your message with words that have the greater effect.

The most effective messages are those expressed with clarity and simplicity. Remember the rule of thumb KISS—Keep It Simple, Speaker. Your message should be delivered through words that make your meaning clear. Using simple, straightforward words and phrases does that best.

If you think to impress people with multisyllabic verbiage, you run the risk of sounding like you're trying to impress people. Worse, your meaning may get muddled, leaving the audience confused about what you're trying to say. It's far more difficult (and impressive) to pack a presentation with meaning by using a few concise, well-chosen words.

Of the words you choose, there is more power in those that are emotive, or evoke an emotional response. The most persuasive presentations (not unlike the most persuasive advertisements) are those that appeal at an emotional level. Emotive words drive a message home with greater force and thus make a presentation more memorable.

Read aloud the words that follow. Which are the more emotive? Police or Gestapo? Happy or delighted? Dead or murdered? Unsafe or hazardous? Morning or dawn? Drug user or junkie? Notice a difference in how you respond?

Emotive words conjure up a "word picture" in the listener's mind. In that respect, they tap into the visual channel of delivery, which gives the verbal channel more depth. Emotive words appeal to people's feelings or senses. In that respect, they're more persuasive.

Sadly, our language is giving way to bland euphemisms. Garbagemen aren't garbagemen anymore; they're sanitation engineers. People hooked on alcohol or drugs aren't drunks or junkies; they're substance abusers. Salespeople are account executives. Mothers are domestic workers. Soon even apple pie will be called something else.

We've adopted terminology that avoids any possibility of ever offending anyone in our pluralistic society. Meanwhile, the richness and power of our language is at risk. Meanings are diluted. Words, once a presenter's sharp-edged tools, are dulled.

Yes, we communicate through vocal and visual channels. Yes, the impact of visual and vocal signals is significant. But words—well chosen and articulated, beautifully intoned—have a power to call forth in the listener's experience sights and sounds and smells and tastes and textures. They can elicit a "gut level" reaction.

Choose words and form phrases that have effect. Avoid the dull. When you present, go for the piercing word, the emotive phrase. Use language that will stir people's feelings and move them to act.

Style

What are you going to do with the visual, vocal, and verbal skills you have developed? Well, of course you present your message through them. But let's say for the sake of discussion that a hundred other people have read this book and are out there applying the same techniques you are. What will distinguish you from them? What will make your presentations stand out?

In a word: style. Style consists of the qualities and characteristics you bring to the platform that no one else can quite duplicate. Every effective speaker projects a memorable style, a distinctive form of presenting that's uniquely their own. Isn't it true the presenters we most enjoy and most remember are those who express their individuality? whose personalities shine through their presentations!

Make a point sometime of observing three notable presenters of our time: Kenneth Blanchard of *One-Minute Manager* fame; Tom Peters, well known for his Excellence and Customer Service series; and Zig Ziglar, author and presenter of "See You at the Top." The information these gentlemen present is not earthshakingly original. (There's very little that is anymore.) The channels through which they communicate are the same ones everyone else uses. They can even be seen to make a mistake on occasion. We all do.

Yet, each one is an optimum presenter. This can be attributed, in part, to their presentation skills. It can also be attributed to style. Each one delivers his message with a personal style that is all his own. Kenneth Blanchard could deliver a presentation on top performance and it wouldn't be the same as Zig Ziglar's. Tom Peters could present on one-minute management and it wouldn't be the same as Mr. Blanchard's. The dimensions of individual personality bring different dimensions to the way a subject is delivered.

Three dimensions, in particular, contribute dramatically to a presentation. They appear in every optimum presenter. They're expressed in the formula $E = E \times 3$.

Effectiveness = The Energy, Enthusiasm, and Encouragement you give to the people in your audience

---

Energy

After a friend had attended a seminar, I asked, "How was it?" She replied (with a wonderfully graphic word picture), "You could watch the grass grow under your feet." That was her way of saying "Ho-hum."

A ho-hum presentation suffers from lethargy. When the minutes tick drearily by like hours, it's a sure sign the presenter needs a good shot in the arm. A shot of *energy*!

How does a presenter convey energy? For starters, get a good night's sleep before you present. (That means you're well prepared in advance so you're not cramming to get ready the night before.) It's awfully hard to energize an audience when you're dragging on your feet, looking at them through blood-shot eyes, or stumbling through your words.

"Psych" yourself up. From the moment you walk out the door in the morning, walk with a lively spring in your step. Swing your arms to get the blood circulating. Envision an upbeat, positive experience. Picture the setting, the audience, and yourself—presenting energetically. Sometimes, just the anticipation will start the adrenalin flowing and produce more energy.

While you're presenting, stay on your feet. Even in more casual, small-group settings, resist the temptation to sit. If you want to keep the audience "up," you need to stay "up." You'll also exude more energy if you're enthused about your subject and not reluctant to show it.

Enthusiasm

Take a moment to complete this questionnaire.

1. Calculate the number of people you come into contact with regularly during an average week. About how many people would that be?

2. Of those people, how many would you describe as enthusiastic?

Whenever I pose those two questions to a group, people respond with numbers like these: out of fifteen or twenty people, one or two are seen as enthusiastic. I never cease to be amazed. We live in the most dynamic country on this planet, and only five percent of the population is enthused?

Sporting events and special occasions excepted, it would appear enthusiasm is sadly lacking. A majority of people don't seem to be happy with who they are, what they're doing, or what they have to say. Or they're not expressing it in ways others observe. Not only is that a shame, in a presenter, it's disastrous! How can you possibly hope to persuade people of the value of your message if you don't express it with enthusiasm?

Enthusiasm is not podium-pounding rhetoric. It's not rah-rah cheerleading or pep-talking. It's simply giving sincere expression to the feeling that you're genuinely interested in your subject and in the people you're addressing. Enthusiasm shows you're delighted with what you're doing and with who you're doing it for.

You enthuse an audience by your enthusiasm. If the topic you're presenting is near and dear to your heart, don't be reluctant to let that show. If it's not, pretend it is. Even if you're presenting what you think is a very dull or difficult subject, look for or create something you can feel enthused about.

Enthusiasm is contagious. Your audience will catch it from you. So when you want people to enjoy—you and your presentation—make it a "special occasion." Deliver it with *enthusiasm*!

Encouragement

I can't think of one situation where a presenter doesn't want the audience encouraged to do something. Sales managers want their reps encouraged to sell the new product. Attorneys want juries encouraged to bring in the right verdict. Teachers and trainers want students encouraged to make use of the information. Practitioners want their peers encouraged to try the new technique. Business people and professionals want their clients encouraged to do business with them. I want you encouraged to present like a pro!

Despite all the information and reasons you may supply, an audience is ultimately encouraged by your confidence. The word *confidence* is derived from *con* ("with") and *fidele* ("faith"). When you deliver your presentation "with faith"—in yourself, in your message, and in your audience—people will be encouraged to take confidence from the confidence you convey.

Part of being an accomplished presenter is being an "encourager." Through a well-prepared presentation that you skillfully deliver while affirming your relationship with your audience, you engender in people the courage to act on your ideas or proposals. When you do, you'll satisfy your objective for presenting in the first place.

Remember the commentary on Fred Astaire that opened this chapter? "He almost always seemed to feel good about himself and enjoy what he was doing. This made his audience enjoy it, too." He had *style*. He presented with energy, enthusiasm, and a confidence that encouraged his audiences to respond favorably, and with applause.

Like every good presenter, he mastered the technicalities first. He prepared and practiced, and over time he perfected the fundamental skills of his art. Once he had those down pat, he was free to dance: to dip and turn and slide across a stage without giving the separate steps a second thought.

Presenting (like dancing) is an art. Skills and techniques do not replace your personal style. Instead, they free you to develop it. When you're not preoccupied with what and how to present, you can more naturally express yourself. Not only will mastery of these skills make your presentations more memorable, but expressing your style will make you more memorable, too.

By Design

Whenever you deliver a presentation, you want to communicate meanings and create impressions by design, not by default. No effective presenter would think of leaving the content of the message to chance. Neither should the elements of delivery be left to chance. That would be like selecting and arranging a gift box with care and then leaving it in the street for someone to come along and pick up. Don't count on the audience to "pick up" the meaning and importance of your message. As the presenter, it's your responsibility to deliver it—with care.

Delivering a presentation with care means investing it with the appropriate verbal, vocal, and visual supports. Every element (words, intonations, movements, attire) is presented with purposeful intent. Variations are woven throughout to maintain interest and attention. And the "package" is delivered with the energy, enthusiasm, and confidence that encourages people to act.

In Chapter 2 on preparing your message, the structure of a presentation was compared to that of a building. The techniques of delivery are the interior furnishings. They add color and comfort and brightness to otherwise nondescript information. Your individual style then adds those personal touches that make the structure uniquely your own and make the visitor feel at home. That's a well-designed presentation.

A Few More Pointers on Delivery

Never read from a script. That's not presenting, it's reading out loud.

Never memorize a script. That's not presenting, it's reciting. Reading or reciting from a script inhibits a natural and expressive delivery. It minimizes rather than optimizes your effectiveness.

Never point at people. It's a rude and potentially offensive gesture. When you gesture to give emphasis to a point, present an open palm with your fingers together (as though you're extending your hand to shake hands with someone.)

Always determine the objective. Whenever you're asked to present to a group, ask, "What's the objective?" (In other words, what outcome do they expect?) The question conveys an interest in the concerns of the audience. More important, you'll gain an insight into how to tailor your presentation to better satisfy your listeners.

Always respect people's time. The second question you should ask is, "How much time have you allowed for my presentation?" If it's too much time or too little time to satisfy the objective, discuss what can be modified: either the time frame or the objective. If the time frame is satisfactory, then prepare a presentation that will run three to five minutes less (shorter if you need to allow time for a question-and-answer period at the end). In that way, you'll be sure to finish within the allotted time.

You may recall the widely reported fiasco that occurred at the 1988

Democratic National Convention. Arkansas Governor Bill Clinton was scheduled to deliver a fifteen-minute speech. He was still talking after half an hour. Teleprompters flashed at him to wrap it up; red lights blinked to get his attention; people in the audience booed and hissed. And still he went on and on. The unfortunate incident was described as "nationally televised political suicide."[4] A long-time, successful career was soured because an otherwise accomplished presenter failed to respect people's time.

Always respect people. Approach your audience with graciousness and good humor. No doubt presenting can be a serious business. You may feel the pressure's really on you to perform. You may think your subject dreadful or dreary. There may be a detractor in the audience. You know the kind. No matter what you say, or how you sound, or how you look, they behave as if they're out to get you. (Don't take it personally. They're not. They look that way at just about everybody because they're poor, miserable creatures.)

Don't let detractors distract you. Focus with good feeling on the rest of your audience, with respect for their time and attention. Look on them as doing you a service by being there and listening to your message. And smile. I smile at people I respect, because I respect the people I like; and the people I like are the same ones who happen to make me smile. That's how I view an audience, and it works.

Always see yourself as a role model (or a potential role model). Whether you present to hundreds of adults at a convention; to a group of senior executives, peers, or employees at the office; or to thirty youngsters in a schoolroom, people are looking at you. Give them sufficient reason to look up to you. Why? Because people are more receptive to those they admire, and thus more readily persuaded by them.

Always say "Thank you" for the opportunity to present. If you're a salesperson who gains access to a customer's office, that's an opportunity. If you're a guest speaker who gains a spot on the agenda, that's an opportunity. If you're a manager, teacher, preacher, or politician who gains access to people's hearts and minds, that's a wonderful opportunity. Whatever your occupation or profession, whatever the occasion of the presentation, receiving people's time and attention should be viewed as a privilege for which you want to say "Thanks!"

To Optimize Your Presentations, Remember

- You deliver your message through three channels of communication.

Visual	Choose appropriate attire and accessories.
	Project a confident posture and demeanor.
	Eye contact, expressions, gestures, and movements add meaning to your message.
Vocal	Develop good vocal qualities and intonation.
	Use intentional pauses.
	Refrain from using fillers (er, um, ah).
Verbal	Use clear, simple, emotive words.

- Whatever you project should:

Fit the setting.
Support your message.
Awaken the audience.
Be done in moderation.

- Present with a style that energizes, enthuses, and encourages.

Reference

1. Marylouise Oates, "It Was the Speech That Ate Atlanta," *Los Angeles Times,* July 22, 1988, pp. 1, 5.

5
Media Make
a Difference

In the fall of 1989, a school district in the San Francisco Bay Area tried out a new program for educating students about the dangers of AIDS. Commenting on its success, a news reporter observed that one sixteen-minute video made a bigger impression on the teens than a whole semester's lectures. (When you can make an impression on teens, that's saying something!)

Since I am a presenter, items like that catch my attention. Understanding the power of audiovisual media, I'm not surprised at the results. What does surprise me is that, given what we've known for so long about the channels of communication, we don't use more of them more effectively. As we discussed in the previous chapter, visual images can have a greater and more lasting impact than words alone.

Of the presentations I've seen, the ones I remember months and years later are those that employed striking audio or visual media. They confirm what Marshall McLuhan proposed in the 1960s: that the medium is the message.

Lynn delivered a presentation aimed at recruiting volunteer workers for clean-up crews at a community festival. She entered the room, rolling ahead of her a large rubber garbage container emblazoned with the festival's logo. Victoria presented a system for disciplining students to a group of elementary school teachers. She set the stage by playing an audiocassette recording of the raucous noises from a grammar school hallway. Andrew stepped to the head of the room with a huge stack of pads and papers and files tied up with red cord. He dropped the stack, breaking the red cord. He presented ways to cut through bureaucratic red tape. He immediately got everyone's attention!

With so many messages vying for people's attention and so many presenters competing for the stage, audiovisuals are one way to imprint your presentation on people's minds. Long after your audience has forgotten the words you've said, they may remember a visual aid or two—provided they're used appropriately.

Audiovisuals as Supporting Material

Before we get into the subject of audiovisuals much further, let me preface this section by emphasizing one point. Audiovisuals are not intended to be your presentation. They're intended to support it. In the effective presentation, audiovisuals are a form of supporting material (see Chapter 2).

Have you ever sat in a meeting when someone delivered a presentation but really didn't present at all? Instead, they stood at the front of the room near an overhead projector, putting up one transparency after another. In a thirty-minute presentation, one minute was taken up with a basic welcome and introduction, one minute was used to close, and the other twenty-eight minutes were used to parade transparency after transparency before your eyes. All too often when this scenario occurs, the overheads are filled with typewritten lines. They may even be duplicates of the very pages you already have in handouts. The person presenting reads. You read along. It's all very exciting and persuasive, right?

Visual aids weren't intended to be used that way. It may be the easiest thing to do. But it doesn't meet the criteria of an effective presentation (AMMA—attention-getting, meaningful, memorable, and activating). It doesn't allow you to present yourself at your best. It doesn't have an impact sufficient to enthuse, energize, or convince the audience. In other words, it's boring.

In addition to being a form of supporting material, audiovisuals are a channel of delivery: verbal, vocal, or visual. As such, they should be created and used in such a way that they satisfy the criteria of effective delivery (see Chapter 4). In other words, they should:

- Fit the setting.
- Support the message.
- Awaken the audience.
- Be used in moderation.

Like your presentation itself, audiovisuals should be attention-getting and meaningful.

Qualities

Audiovisuals that satisfy that standard (and audiences) are pictorial, colorful, and creative. They add to the presentation of a subject a fresh and unique treatment in sight or sound. Properly used, they visually magnify or audibly amplify the meaning in your message.

To illustrate: While doing some work with a company, I sat in on a number of presentations given by salespeople on their action plans for the year. The first sales rep began with a transparency that looked like this:

```
        Objective

Product      Forecast

Widgets        2200
Gadgets         780
Woofers        1010
```

The next rep followed with a transparency that resembled this one:

```
        Objective

Product      Forecast

Widgets         900
Gadgets        1500
Woofers         375
```

The third rep stepped up and began with a transparency in brilliant colors that looked something like this:

```
    Objective
```

He then presented how much he'd have to sell in order to acquire the boat of his dreams. To achieve his objective would mean meeting aggressive sales goals, a point not lost on the managers listening. That's an example of approaching a mundane subject in a creative, attention-getting, and memorable way that distinguishes you from the routine presenter.

Pictorial

Visual aids are meant to be just that: visual. Not verbal, not numeric, but visual. Key points or supporting material are depicted in forms that augment your words: expressive or vivid photos, graphs, charts, or illustrations. They are the pictures worth a thousand words.

Words are not visualizations. They're simply lines and squiggles on a page. Therefore, visual aids that display mostly words are not really visual aids. They're just media reproductions of those same lines and squiggles.

The value in presenting information pictorially was confirmed in a course I taught on communication. During the first class we covered the elements of a communication situation: people, setting, messages, channels, norms, noise, and feedback. I formed the class into seven small groups. Each group was assigned one element to discuss and depict in a visual aid which they then presented to the class at large.

Each group drew a picture or visual symbol that captured the nature of their topic. The results were noteworthy. When the class was tested a few weeks later, the majority remembered all seven elements. Some of the test papers had little drawings sketched in the margins. The students recalled the elements based on those visuals more than they would have recalled verbal descriptions alone.

Decades ago presenters may have produced "visual" aids that consisted primarily of words because the process of creating any other kind was too costly, too time consuming, or too tedious—especially if you had to prepare them yourself. Today, however, with the technology that's available, preparing interesting, pictorial visual aids is much easier than it used to be.

It's also almost expected nowadays. People are accustomed to seeing information graphically displayed: on computers, on video screens, on television, in newspapers, in the business press, and in professional journals. And in other people's presentations. If you don't depict the highlights of your message pictorially, you'll be one of the few who doesn't.

Colorful

A second factor that always makes for more dynamic visuals is color. Color has been described as "the powerful persuader." An issue of *The Board Report for Graphic Artists*[1] detailed several advantages to color, noting that "we can expect color to effect responses....Color appeals to emotions....The right colors can promote attention, evoke moods, create desire and even generate a favorable response." (Conversely, the wrong colors can generate a negative response: so watch what colors you wear and what colors you use in visual aids.)

Market research and scientific studies on the effects of color have found that we associate colors with different characteristics. Furthermore, the association is often based on gender. Studies have found, for example, that men typically associate red with passion and excitement, which explains why many men prefer red in a sports car. Women, on the other hand, associate red with romance and fulfillment, which explains why red roses are popular with so many women. Gallup Poll surveys of color preferences by gender offer these further insights. In order of retention: men best remember violet, dark blue, olive green, and yellow. Women best remember dark blue, olive green, yellow, and red.

According to the Board Report, these are meanings we commonly associate with different colors.

Black	authority, death, strength, loyalty, mystery
Blue	faith, cold, award, truth, tenderness
Brown	action, earthiness, autumn, fellowship
Green	envy, health, friendship, leisure, youthfulness
Red	passion, heat, excitement, love, fulfillment
Orange	warmth, action, power, valor, aggression, fury
Purple	dignity, royalty, frugality, melancholy
White	holiness, cleanliness, purity, professionalism
Yellow	confidence, knowledge, esteem, playfulness

We also attach symbolic meanings to color. On a graph of income and expenses, for example, earnings would be depicted in green (the color of money), while costs would be depicted in red (a color we associate with debt). We use phrases like "looking at the world through rose-colored glasses" to describe someone with an optimistic outlook and "I'm blue" to convey a mood of depression.

Successful marketeers apply this color information all the time. Blue is associated with faith and truth, and it's well remembered. White is associated with cleanliness and professionalism. It's not surprising, then, to see white-collar professionals favoring dark-blue suits and white shirts. A majority of fast-food restaurants feature combinations of yellow, orange, and brown. They're the colors we associate with confidence and playfulness, warmth and action, and fellowship. They're the colors of harvest—of food. From the colors in commercials that promote products, to the colors used in packaging their goods, people who want to sell something know the value of the right color choices.

Whether our responses to colors are physiologically, emotionally, or culturally formed is, for our purposes, a moot point. For presenters, the value of understanding the effects of colors lies in the high degree of impact they have on people. We view the world in color, not black and white. We remember some colors better than others. We associate colors with certain characteristics or symbolic meanings. And we often buy ideas (not just products) on the basis of how they're packaged. It's an important point to keep in mind next time you "package" your presentation in visual aids (including your own attire).

Colors are also attention-getters. The Board Report cited above points out that "a Newspaper Advertising Bureau report states that reading of the body copy in an ad increased by eighty percent when color was added." (Imagine that statistic depicted in a bar chart. See how dramatic that would be?) If the same holds true for visual aids, your presentation can be made much more memorable with the simple addition of color. The right colors.

Creative

In recent months I've attended enough presentations to see enough bar graphs, line graphs, and pie charts to last a lifetime. Charts are fast replacing the old typewritten transparency as the most overused visual aid around. Not that I have anything against charts. There are times when they're the most logical choice to support the material presented.

However, there's a danger in overusing anything. After a while it becomes meaningless. It fails to hold people's interest or have the impact it once did when it was new. That's true of cars. It's true of space flights. And it's true of charts and graphs. So be careful not to use charts and graphs to excess. Think of other ways you might get the message across.

Be creative. Use your imagination. Ask yourself: What will spark the audience's interest and at the same time be relevant to my message? What innovative forms or media can I use to express this theme or point in a way that's unique, that's different from the norm?

As a person who observes presentations, I'm delighted when I see people present information and ideas creatively. It says something about the kind of thought presenters have given to communicating their message. They're generally the ones (the presenters and the visuals) that audiences most remember.

The pages that follow discuss some of the more commonly used audiovisuals and newer media options as well. Some work better in some settings than they do in others. All have advantages and limitations. What you choose to use should be guided by the criteria and qualities outlined earlier in this chapter.

Low Tech

Years ago there was a saying that circulated among a group of us: "Have flip chart, will travel." We'd fold up our portable tripods, slip our charts into vinyl cases, and we'd be off and running to the next presentation. In the context of the technologies available today, the flip chart is an endangered species. All the same, it still has its uses, as do other "low tech" visual aids.

Old Standbys

Flip Charts.   A flip chart is little more than an oversized note pad. As such, it's used in smaller group settings and can be presented interactively or proactively.

When used interactively, charts arc developed as you go along. You present a point, write it down (or draw it), and note responses elicited from the group. Used this way, they're still one of the best aids in instructional settings and planning sessions where the presenter plays the role of facilitator. The material can be reinforced for the group if people are provided with handouts in an outline format that leaves sufficient room for notes. If it's appropriate to the situation, arrange to have the flip charts transcribed and copies distributed to participants as a further reminder of the presentation.

Presented proactively, flip charts are prepared in advance. They're created to provide an outline of your message, guiding you through the points you want to cover. They should be prepared by a professional, or at least someone with good illustration and penmanship skills. Dog-eared flip charts filled with sloppy writing on uneven lines can detract from a presentation. The most common applications for using prepared charts are marketing or announcement presentations, where the format and content of the presentation is predetermined. Used in this way, they're a visual aid that helps you more than the audience.

Some situations benefit from both: one prepared set of flip charts for proactive presentation and a second chart of blank sheets. For example, in a product announcement meeting you may present the first part of the program proactively using prepared charts. The second chart would be used to note responses you elicit from the group about, say, applications or prospects for the new product.

Whether charts are prepared or blank, follow the rule of three: not more than two or three points per sheet. Too many points on any one page will give charts a cluttered appearance and detract from their readability. So will used, dried up marking pens that don't make a bold impression. Start your presentation with a supply of fresh, new pens in hand. (Just like copiers always seem to run out of paper just when you're ready to use the machine, marking pens left on a flip chart stand always seem to run out of ink just when you want to use them.) When you use fresh pens, ink may bleed from one sheet to the next. You can avoid this by stapling two sheets together at the bottom corners (although you'll use twice as much paper when you do).

The advantages to flip charts are that they're portable and therefore convenient to use. Obviously, you can set up a flip chart just about anywhere, without regard for electrical outlets or special equipment. And they can be personalized to the audience and the situation.

Although economy was also considered an advantage, that's no longer as true as it once was. Paper is not an inexpensive medium anymore. And the way some people go through reams of charts—especially in interactive settings where they're used only once—the cost can mount up. With the technology that's available today, other types of visual aids can be prepared more easily and relatively inexpensively.

The single greatest limitation to flip charts is that they tend to be a word-oriented medium. Unless the presenter has an artistic bent or the charts were prepared in advance by an illustrator, the impact of meaningful pictures and colors is lost. This can be overcome by combining the use of flip charts with other forms of audiovisual aids.

Visual Boards. Like flip charts, visual boards are most appropriate in smaller-group interactive settings where the board is the medium on which to note your points and the audience's responses. The same limitation applies: they tend to be a word-dominated medium.

Visual boards include blackboards, green boards, brown boards, and white boards, either bolted to the wall or portable. If wall space permits, it's useful to have three or four movable boards mounted on rails, especially in conference and training rooms. In this way, the presenter can alternately expose or conceal different boards.

The most versatile visual boards are white and magnetized. Visual boards that are magnetized allow even more flexibility to develop a creative visual presentation. Pictures, symbols, cut-outs, and labeled strips of colorful poster board can be made up with magnetic strip tape for backing. They can be put up on the board one by one and moved to illustrate different arrangements of material.

I observed one presentation on a distributed data processing system that used a magnetic board effectively. The presenter convincingly displayed the advantages of the system, not so much by words as by visually demonstrating varying configurations. Each component of the system was represented by a magnetized piece, which could be placed at any point on the board.

Another device that's gaining in popularity is the electronic visual board. It combines the write-on surface of a visual board with photocopier technology. Electronic visual boards are especially useful in small-group meetings, planning sessions, and instructional programs. After writing on the board, you can advance the panel. With the push of a button, copies can be made and distributed to the group.

Overhead Transparencies. Useful in both proactive and interactive modes, transparencies offer several advantages over flip charts and visual boards. For one, they can be projected onto a large overhead screen that can be viewed by a much larger audience.

For another, they can be recycled. Visual boards get erased. Flip charts get marked on and dog-eared. But transparencies can be marked and erased. Using transparency marking pens, you can write on them, highlight items, or circle points you want to emphasize—and wipe the slate clean when you're through. You can use the same transparencies dozens of times and erase any writing you've done so they look like new.

Transparencies have been the object of some criticism, which isn't so much the fault of the medium as it is of the way it is often used. If a transparency is a duplication of typewritten material, then it doesn't meet the criteria of an effective visual aid. (It's verbal, not visual.) In addition, information-bound presenters often read verbatim from transparencies, instead of presenting them as supporting material. But these misuses aside, transparencies can be a good presentation tool.

Nowadays, professional-looking, colorful, pictorial transparencies can be created easily and economically. The master copy can be prepared by a novice using transfer type, paste-ups, or computer-generated data: bold type, charts, graphs, even illustrations. Or source material can be used: photographs, maps, excerpts from magazines. With the features available on photocopiers, the master copy can be reproduced right onto a transparency. It can be enlarged, reduced, and prepared in color. You can end up with sharp, creative images and an effective visual aid.

Transparencies can also be personalized more easily than many other media. You can start with the master copy of a transparency you use repeatedly from one presentation to another. Add names, a photograph, a company logo, or an excerpt from an annual report. In the time it takes to run a piece of paper through a copier, you have a customized transparency.

Tape overhead transparencies to cardboard frames (available at office or art supply stores). Frames make transparencies easier to handle (they won't cling together), and help preserve them for repeated use. They also give you a margin around the transparency. So what? So you can make notations of points you want to be sure to address. Write quotations, percentages, references to names or examples on the border of a frame. As you place the transparency on the projector glass, a quick glance at your notes will refresh your memory.

Two physical limitations can detract from the use of transparencies if you haven't set up the facilities with care. The arm of the overhead projector may block someone's view. This can be avoided by setting the projector down on a lower-level stand and tilting the lens-mirror upward to project the transparency at a higher viewing height.

The second limitation may be more difficult to control since it has to do with lighting in the room. Transparencies project a sharper image in a dimly lit room. I'm reluctant to darken a room completely since it inhibits contact with the audience. If the facilities permit, simply dim the lights or turn off just one panel.

If you're using transparencies as you should—as a supporting visual aid—you won't be displaying them all the time. Turn the overhead projector off when it's not in use so the light isn't a distraction to the audience.

Display Items

Poster Boards.   When professionally prepared, poster boards are a quality way to display material. They offer the same portability as flip charts, but with more durability. They're best used for sign boards or for mounted design drawings, renderings, or photographs that wouldn't display as well on overhead transparencies or in slides.

Because of the cost and quality of preparation, they're not a visual aid you use interactively. In other words, you don't write on poster boards. And given their limited size, they're most appropriate for use in smaller groups.

The most notable limitation to poster boards is that they can be awkward to handle. Obviously they don't flip easily as flip charts do, and too many can be weighty as well. Suppose you have three boards stacked on an easel. You refer to the first board. Now what do you do? Lift it and slide it behind the other two (which, because of their weight, may tip forward and fall)? Lean it against a wall? You see the problem. (Imagine if you had eight or ten boards to contend with!)

Because of this handling factor, poster boards are most suitable when just two or three boards will suffice. When a presentation lends itself to the boards being continuously displayed, each should be propped on a separate easel.

Models. A visual aid that's often overlooked, models can be a creative way to support your presentation. Architects and real estate developers have understood for years the advantages to using models. They're three-dimensional so they convey the depth and proportion of the real thing. They provide color, variety, texture, and feeling. They're literally a hands-on kind of visual aid.

Portability, cost, and the time to produce a model are factors to be considered. While some models are stationary, very expensive, and time-consuming to make, all models need not be. Cardboard mock-ups can be created, for example, to illustrate certain products or objects.

On one occasion, I attended a seminar presented by a chiropractor who used a model of a spine (a fixture he no doubt kept around his clinic). At the end of his presentation, he distributed key chains to members of the audience—attached to a small replica of a spine. He very effectively capitalized on the use of his model by putting a miniaturized version in every person's hand. That's one way to make a visual model, and your presentation, more memorable.

Props. While a model is a miniature or representation made to scale, a prop is symbolic. Any object that depicts some characteristic of your message can be used. The intent is for the audience to associate a principle of your presentation with the prop. One prop I use, for example, is a colorfully wrapped and ribboned box to convey the point that delivering a presentation is like giving someone a special gift.

I've seen presenters use balloons, footballs, coins, chairs, mobiles, and even their podiums as props. Props can gain the audience's attention and provide a creative "memory hook" for the message. They can be portable, colorful, inexpensive, and used in a variety of settings and ways. But props can also be misused. If not carefully chosen and effectively related to the message, they can appear gimmicky or superfluous.

Media

Audio Recordings. When sound is the subject of a presentation or sound effects can add to it, audio recordings can be effective. I've seen (or rather heard) audiocassette recordings used to compare dialogue in a presentation on interaction skills; to support a presentation on sub-liminal music; and (as noted in an earlier example) to set the stage for a presentation that addressed classroom teachers. Generally, though, au-dio recordings are somewhat limited in their applications. And audio alone doesn't have as great an impact on people as the visual channel of delivery does.

There are two main considerations when using audio recordings. First, the sound system should be adequate for the setting. A portable cassette player might work fine in a small room, but it will hardly do in a convention center. Second, since the presenter has nothing to do while the recording is played, good timing and demeanor are essential. You need to have the recording all set up and ready to go. When it's time to use it, turn it on, step aside, and stand by in a poised manner as the audience listens. Then, turn it off and resume your presentation—all without a hitch. If the volume is too loud or too soft, if the recording is muffled or scratchy, intervening to correct these problems will inter-rupt the flow of your presentation.

Slides.   Unlike other audiovisuals, slides can be presented simulta-neously on multiple screens, with an accompanying sound track of voice or background music. Multiscreen slide presentations can create capti-vating and entertaining special effects. Because they require special fa-cilities and talent to create, they're most often seen in high-budget train-ing centers, conventions, and trade shows. A multiscreen presentation isn't supporting material for a stand-up presenter. It's the presentation itself.

Single-screen slide presentations, however, can be put together by anyone who presents. And with the benefits of modern technology, they can be done on a moderate budget.

Slides are an especially good visual for creating the perception of high quality and a professional approach to presenting. They're color-ful and project sharp images. They're very easy to use. They're adapt-able to a variety of settings. And slides can be customized, selected, and rearranged to suit the requirements of different presentations.

Films and Videotapes.   The advantages of films and videotapes are numerous. Providing both audio and visual support, they take advan-tage of every channel of delivery. Most are professionally prepared and therefore add to the impression of a quality program. They're generally adaptable to both large audiences and small-group settings.

In addition, films and videotapes are an "active" medium, projecting people and events in action. Other media, like flip charts, transparen-cies, or slides, are "passive" by comparison. As an active medium, films and videotapes can take an audience to places and involve them in a way not possible with other visual aids. In that respect, films or videotapes can have tremendous impact on an audience.

For example, I use a videotape to support a presentation on motivating employees. It develops analogies with a sports team. You are there as the U.S. hockey team wins the gold medal at Lake Placid. The videotape conveys the excitement of being a winner as no transparency, slide, or flip chart can. People walk out of that presentation wanting to excel.

While films or videotapes can add a lot to presentations given in an interactive mode, naturally there's no interaction occurring while the picture is being viewed. To make the most of film and videotape support, you must comment on key points afterward. Most of the films and videotapes distributed for business purposes include leader's guides, which offer helpful ideas for facilitating group discussion.

Videotapes offer an advantage over films in that they're more convenient to use. No figuring out how to wind the filmstrip through a 1930s projector! However, with videotapes you need to make sure that the screen image will be large enough for the whole group to view, which depends on the equipment that's available.

One potential drawback with films and videotapes is that they're canned. If your presentation would benefit from personalization (as in sales or client-specific situations), be sure to show the relationship of what the customer has seen to the customer's situation. Or combine the use of film or videotapes with other visual aids that are customized.

High Tech

Technological advances have produced a whole new range of audiovisual choices for presenters. Have you ever found yourself thinking, "What, me create transparencies for a presentation? I don't have any artistic talent!" Or, "I can't use slides. It takes a week to get them back from the photo lab and I'm doing this presentation on Friday!" The good news is that those old assumptions no longer hold true. You can create dynamic visuals. And you can have them by tomorrow.

Many computer users are familiar with the term *CAD* (computer-assisted drafting). Well, welcome to *CAP*—computer-assisted presentations. Anyone who has access to a personal computer can now prepare professional quality visual aids easily and economically. You can create transparencies and slides (and accompanying handouts for the audience) that will make people sit up and take notice.

The best of the presentation graphics software that's on the market today enables you to produce every type of visual imaginable using a computer keyboard and screen. The computer generates labels, titles, line drawings, charts and graphs of all kinds, freehand drawings and illustrations. Business symbols and mapping options are available. Graphics can be produced from data that resides in an existing spreadsheet program. And desktop presentations can be delivered right from the computer screen.

Color printers produce master copies for high-quality transparencies. And computer data files can be converted to 35-mm color slides within twenty-four hours. Thankfully, the days of dull visuals are over! Thankfully, the tedium of preparing them is, too.

I would like to tell you, "Go and buy this." I won't. Technologies and vendors change too rapidly. In the time that elapses between my writing this book and your reading it, more computer companies will have come and gone and new versions of software will be on the market. If you can make use of presentation graphics software (and you can if you make presentations), then I recommend this: Proceed in the same manner as you would if you were buying a new car. In other words, check a few of the lots around town and take a test drive first.

You can find the computer software that's right for you if you follow a few simple steps.

1. Determine your needs. What types of presentations do you make? What kind of material and data are you dealing with? What capabilities do you need in a computer software program: lettering, graphs, charts, freehand drawing, symbols, customization, connectivity with other programs, production of photographic slides?

2. Shop the shops. Go to at least two reputable dealers. Ask them to recommend the top two or three presentation graphics programs. Compare product functions and specifications in relation to your needs.

3. View comparative demonstrations of the products. Ask to see printed samples. If the software publisher makes a trial or demonstration diskette available, try that out first.

4. Ask for the names of at least three installed users as references. Talk to them. Ask about training, ease of use, ongoing support, and the functional advantages and limitations of the software. What actual users have experienced is far more reliable than any promotional literature you'll read.

A Word of Caution.   As volatile as the computer industry is, you're far better off spending a little more money for a recognized name-brand system than you are choosing something because it's a good deal. Remember the old adage, "If it's too good to be true, it is." There's a lot of hardware and software collecting dust on shelves because people bought an inexpensive, "off-the-wall" system produced by a start-up company that went out of business.

One Last Point. Presentation graphics software is a boon to presenters. However, don't get carried away. The audience came to see and hear you. And the occasion of your presentation gives you an opportunity to make yourself known and be heard. The success of your presentation doesn't lie solely in projecting whiz-bang graphics (although they can add to its impact and appeal). It still lies primarily in your relational skills: in how well you relate, and relate your message, to people.

A Case in Point. If what people wanted was information, they could pick up the newspaper, business publications, or watch television. If what people wanted was to hear the information from a recognized authority, they could rent any number of videotapes that feature Ph.D.s and watch them at their convenience. But they don't. They attend meetings, seminars, conferences, training sessions, and guest speaker appearances, and they do so with anticipation. What they want is to hear from a warm body who delivers a meaningful message and delivers it with personal presence.

By all means, make use of quality visuals that enhance your presentation. Just don't hide behind them or expect them to carry the day.

Creation and Use

I assess a presentation from the standpoint of whether it's "high stakes" or "low stakes." The more I have at stake, the more I'll invest in the audiovisuals I use to support the presentation. It doesn't make any sense to spend $795 on a videotape rental for a presentation to a client whose order will yield $100 in commissions. Conversely, it doesn't make any sense to use cheap, tacky flip charts with a group that has considerable influence.

The deciding factor isn't always money. The time and effort you put into audiovisuals, the exposure you'll have when you present, the perceptions you want to create and the corporate image you need to project: they're all considerations, too. But when you do get around to choosing the audiovisuals you're going to use, you can go hog-wild or low budget. Which is it going to be? Apply the principle of return on investment (ROI). It gives you a benchmark to decide how much to do with audiovisual aids.

Original or Prepared

Once you've determined what a reasonable investment is, you can either create your own original visuals or obtain media that's already prepared. If you create your own, take advantage of current technologies: presentation graphics software, desktop publishing equipment, photocopiers that reduce and enlarge images and produce copies in full color. If equipment isn't available at your workplace, it is at many copy and duplicating services and print shops.

Art supply stores are another good place to check out. Not only will you find basic supplies (flip charts, poster board, marking pens, and so on), but looking around can stir your creative thinking. Look through the transfer-type symbols, logos, caricatures, and border designs. Glance through the catalogs of illustrations and paste-ups. They can trigger ideas for creative visuals.

If you're looking for audiovisuals that are already prepared, the first place to check is your own inventory. Most large organizations have audiovisuals of all types already in stock. In addition, films and videotapes on virtually any subject are available through a number of outside sources. Check the film and videotape departments of your local library or university. National distributors of films, videotapes, and audiocassettes also offer selections for purchase or rent.

Some presentations benefit from the creation of customized visuals, notably, sales and customer-specific presentations. Visuals like slides and transparencies can be appropriately personalized by adding the company slogan, logo, an image of their building, or the names of specific departments or personnel.

Customizing can also be appropriate for in-house presentations. On one occasion, I was asked to help with a company supervisors' meeting. The manager was especially concerned about building morale and teamwork. We collected still photographs of the supervisors and workers at their jobs at the various company sites. From those, a local video production company created a commercial-quality videotape that incorporated the company logo and screen titles. Because no on-site filming was required, the tape was produced at a nominal cost. And it had just the effect on the group that the manager wanted. Customizing a videotape provided a meaningful, upbeat, captivating opening to his presentation.

How You Present Them

Once you've created or selected your audiovisuals, you want to present them effectively. Be sure you're familiar with the medium and comfortable working with it. Do a "walk through" of your presentation beforehand to ensure that your materials are set up in the proper order and that you have your timing down pat.

When you present visual aids, be conscious of where and how you stand in relation to the audience, and whether you can maintain eye contact with them. With flip charts and visual boards, take care not to turn your back on the audience. Cultivate the skill of writing from the side so you can stay half-turned toward the group.

With transparencies, don't stand as though affixed to the overhead projector. Don't look down at the surface of the projector and read the transparency verbatim. (The audience can do that for themselves.) Instead, step back and stand beside the screen. (You can always step forward again when you want to switch to the next transparency.) Refer to the projection on the screen, and summarize or highlight the key points. In this way, you retain the audience's attention by continuing to focus on them.

As effective as they can be, slides, films, and videotapes have two potential drawbacks. You're usually at the side or back of the room, and the room is usually dark. If possible, dim the lights rather than turn them off completely. (Darkened rooms are all the encouragement some people need to drop off to sleep.) When you show slides, if you're narrating the presentation, do so from the side of the audience up toward the front of the room. Again, it helps you sustain some degree of contact with the group.

Pitfalls to Avoid

In this era of electronic and computer technologies, there's no excuse for not making good use of dynamic audiovisuals that enhance your presentation. The key is enhance. To use media support effectively, you must avoid some common pitfalls.

Distractions.   Take care not to use a pointer, medium, or equipment in ways that distract the audience. Combining different forms of audiovisuals can be effective. Using sophisticated graphics technologies can be impressive. They can also be disastrous. Multimedia presentations run the risk of presenting too much media and too little you. As projections change, screens flash, and equipment is turned on and off, the audience can be distracted from the real reason they're there. Remember: Use audiovisuals in moderation.

Blocking the View.   The placement of audiovisual equipment and media should be such that everyone in the audience has a clear view. Keep obstacles that might block the audience's view out of the way—including you.

   Where you stand in relation to the visuals you're projecting is important. Position yourself so that you avoid blocking someone's view, while at the same time maintain visual contact with the audience. When transparencies or slides are projected on a screen, don't cross the path of the projection. Doing so throws your shadow up on the screen and creates a visual disruption.

Too Much, Too Long. Avoid delivering a presentation primarily through audiovisual media. Doing so minimizes your opportunities to relate personally to the audience. Anything done to excess will tire people out or bore them. And you won't persuade people if they're tired or bored.

Too Much on Too Little.   More is not always better. Don't expect your audience to try to decipher cluttered or complex visuals. You have to make it easy for them if you want to keep their attention. Far better to have five transparencies with three words apiece than one transparency with fifteen.

Too Many Words, Not Enough Pictures.   Far better still to use a visual with one meaningful and memorable illustration: a drawing, a picture, a chart, a graph—whatever pictorializes the point. Words should be scarce on visuals, and they should be used primarily to label, highlight, or summarize.

Dullness.   Brighten your visuals with vibrant, meaningful colors. But, again, more is not better. Limit the number of colors you use to not more than three per visual.

Failing to Check in Advance.   Short of falling flat on your face, nothing interrupts the flow of a presentation more than the unexpected. The avoidable "unexpected" shouldn't occur to a professional presenter. Thus you should avoid some common mishaps: light switches or electrical outlets that can't be found, equipment cords that aren't long enough, equipment light bulbs that burn out, marking pens that run out of ink. Always check out facilities, equipment, and supplies ahead of time. And always carry extras with you: extra equipment bulbs, extra marking pens, and a long extension cord.

Gimmicks.   When you're good, you don't need gimmicks. You'll keep people's attention and give them a meaningful, memorable experience when you skillfully deliver a well-prepared message. Avoid tricks or surprises. You're not a comedian, a huckster, or a carnival barker, and you don't want to be perceived as one.

I remember the best presenters I've ever seen. I remember the worst ones, too. Like word-of-mouth advertising: it goes both ways. One of the better presenters I've heard quickly turned into one of the worst because he didn't avoid this pitfall.

It occurred at a marketing conference I attended with a couple of business associates who thought I'd enjoy the featured speaker. He was dynamite when he first stepped up and addressed the crowd. You could almost feel people straighten up in their seats as he enlivened them and captured their attention. He started to deliver a slide presentation. And then, a hush fell over the room. Flashed up on the screen, ever so briefly (but noticeably), was a slide that was completely out of context— and potentially offensive to some people. He risked his presentation for a gimmick.

When you want to be perceived as a credible professional, leave the gimmicks to someone who isn't.

To Present Audiovisuals Like a PRO, Remember

- Audiovisuals are supporting material that should:

    Fit the setting.
    Support the message.
    Awaken the audience.
    Be used in moderation.

- Effective media messages are:

  Pictorial.
  Colorful.
  Creative.

Reference

1. "Color: The Powerful Persuader," *The Board Report for Graphic Artists,* Drew Allen Miller, Publisher, February 1985, unpaged.

6
Overcoming Anxiety

You have worksheets to simplify outlining a presentation. That's fine. You now understand some techniques for relating to the audience. Great. You're aware of how to project yourself, and you've gained some ideas about media. That's all well and good. But what in the world do you do about the fear that grips you at the prospect of speaking before a group? Never mind actually doing it. Just thinking about doing it makes your palms sweat.

You may be a highly skilled professional, confident in your craft. You may have no difficulty dealing with individuals on a one-on-one basis. You may be a dynamo when it comes to negotiating. But step up in front of a group (especially your peers!), and mysteriously (but, oh so predictably) you feel anxious.

If that's not true for you, you're in the minority. (You can save some time and go on to Chapter 7.)

If it is true for you, you have a lot of company. Anxiety about speaking in public is so prevalent that surveys have shown it's something a majority of people fear most. So, what do you do about it?

Well, you have two choices. You can succumb to your anxiety and never present again. Of course, chances are you'll limit your career. You'll miss opportunities other less qualified people may capture. And you'll forego an avenue for demonstrating leadership. You'll also miss out on what can become a very gratifying experience.

Your other choice? Understand your anxiety and overcome it. So much work has been done in recent years in the area of human behavior that there are now techniques—simple, proven, workable techniques—that enable people to overcome anxieties. Doing so has numerous advantages. As we proceed through this chapter, I encourage you to reflect on the advantages to presenting and to make a commitment to overcome what inhibits you.

A Matter of Ability

As a veteran presenter, there are times when I still "choke." Every once in a while when I'm about to present, my throat gets tight, my palms get clammy, and my heart starts to pound. Is that fear of speaking before a group?

I'd labeled it "fear" because I was experiencing the symptoms of what's described as "fear of public speaking." Then, during television coverage of the 1988 Winter Olympics, an announcer related an incident that put this so-called fear in its proper perspective.

A world-class figure skater was in the lead after the preliminary rounds. But when it came time for her to perform in the finals, she refused to go on. It seems she'd fallen several times during recent competitions. As a result, she dreaded going out on the ice and "presenting" her routine in front of all those people. She was fearful she'd fall again. Her coach pleaded with her. Her parents pleaded with her. Then finally, they called in a friend.

Imagine, he said, going into a very exclusive French restaurant, the kind that doesn't show prices on the menu. You reach into your pockets and they're empty. You have nothing to cover the cost of a meal, much less one in this place. You get up to leave, afraid you'll get caught.

Now, imagine going into that same restaurant again. Only this time, you reach into your pockets and discover you have a hundred dollar bill. Well, you'll take a chance and order. You're a little nervous since you are not sure you have enough to cover the whole tab. You probably do. You're just not sure.

That hundred dollars, the skater's friend explained, represented her ability. Ability gained through training. Ability gained from practice and experience. That ability gave her a reason to take a stab at it, to give it a try. Not being sure if your ability is enough "to cover the whole tab" would make anyone nervous. But that's all. It wasn't fear that kept her from going on, he assured her. Just nerves. Encouraged, the skater went out, presented her routine, and walked away with the gold!

One person goes out boldly to present. Another does not. The only difference between them is this: the person who presents remembers the bill in their pocket while the "stay at home" does not. The ones who present understand what they're feeling isn't fear but a simple case of nerves. They recognize it for what it really is, confront it, and go on.

The others succumb to what they perceive to be fear and are disabled by it.

The only thing standing between you and the "gold" is affirming (and further developing) the ability you have. Every person I've ever met has an ability to present. Sure, some demonstrate more skill than others because they've had more training and practice. But everyone has the basic ability. You have the ability.

When I'm getting ready for what I think of as a high-stakes presentation (the kind that makes me nervous), I slip a crisp one hundred dollar bill into my pocket. I may have to cash it in to buy groceries on the way home. But for the time that I'm presenting, it's an encouraging reminder that I have "a-bill-ity." (Next time you're asked to give a presentation, make a trip to the bank first!)

Worst Case, Best Case

To calculate the risks in a situation, I do a worst-case, best-case scenario. When it comes to presenting, the worst isn't all that bad.

There are risks associated with presenting, no doubt. You might forget an important point you wanted to make. (Chances are the audience won't know it unless you showed them your model outline beforehand.) You might have a detractor in the audience who makes you feel uncomfortable. (Chances are they're the kind of person who makes everyone feel uncomfortable.) You might not present perfectly. Aha, there's the real crux of it! (Well, nobody ever does.)

We make presenting out to be worse than it actually is by conjuring up what terrible things might happen. The fact that they rarely, if ever, do happen is irrelevant. This is an emotional issue, rooted in our perceptions (and we all know how powerful they can be). If we're going to look forward to presenting as something better rather than worse, we need to square our perceptions with the facts.

I suspect that somewhere in the recesses of our minds, we harbor an image of audiences throwing rotten vegetables at vaudeville performers who didn't do well. The environment in which you present may seem as wild and crazy as a vaudeville theater. But, the fact is, in over twenty years of presenting and attending presentations, I've never once seen a rotten vegetable thrown.

Okay, you say, you really have more at stake than that. You present to senior executives and the way you present is critical to your career success. You're in a profession that mandates making effective presentations; your livelihood depends on it. You present in meetings with peers and employees and you need to demonstrate your competence.

Those are all valid reasons for being interested in how well you present. But view them as motivators rather than inhibitors, that foster anxiety. They can prompt you to deal with the jitters and concentrate on your abilities instead. After all, the very fact that you're in a position to present suggests you have ability (or you wouldn't be called on to speak).

What's the best case? I think the very best that can happen is that someone or something will be changed as a result of what and how you present. Someone will be so moved or impressed by what you've said that they'll go out and actually do something with it. You will have had influence. You will have made a difference.

I've seen it happen time and again with people I've worked with. I remember, in particular, "B." B. has a son who's a hemophiliac. With the onslaught of AIDS, her son (like all hemophiliacs) is at risk. She became personally committed to getting the message out to the community: to educate people and appeal to them for support. During the course of a month, she developed a presentation that went from mediocre to marvelously moving. When she made her final presentation to a group, there wasn't a dry eye in the room (including mine). Whenever she has an opportunity to present, B. will make a difference in people's lives.

The difference you can make may have to do with improving your business or your income. It may relate to improving youngsters' learning or adult education. It may have to do with bringing about a change in community or political affairs. Whatever it is you happen to be interested in or concerned with, by presenting you can make a difference. Isn't that reason to overcome a momentary case of nerves?

Stages

Overcoming anxiety about presenting occurs through a process with three stages. They don't necessarily occur in the order listed. Sometimes they come about concurrently. Sometimes it takes only one or two.

Acknowledge the Source

Usually, the process starts by acknowledging the source of our anxiety. We can better confront and dissolve the jitters when we understand what causes them and when we see anxiety for what it really is.

Most of the people I deal with are bright and articulate. They're well-educated, experienced, and talented business and professional people.

Many have credentials that would put my own to shame. Based on their abilities, there's no logical, rational reason for them to dread presenting (especially since we've already confirmed you run no risk of being pelted with rotten vegetables).

So, if people aren't anxious about presenting for logical, rational reasons, the source of anxiety must be emotional or psychological. Now, I'm no psychologist and I have no interest in dabbling in pop psychology. There are enough people around who do that. I don't need to throw my hat into the ring. But it doesn't take a genius to observe that we live in a culture that puts people under pressure. Pressure to be more. Pressure to do more. Pressure to have more.

Recruiting ads tout, "Be all you can be!" Product commercials flaunt the brawny and beautiful. Self-improvement books and seminars echo the message. We're exposed daily—not to what we are—but to what we are not! You may have a hundred dollar bill in your pocket, but some snooty waiter's trying to convince you that you're broke!

None of us are, yet, all we can be. Few of us are brawny or beautiful enough to pass an audition for casting in a movie role. But in view of the mass of media messages influencing our perceptions, it's not surprising more people don't jump for joy at the prospect of appearing before a group. Why? Because they feel self-conscious.

The bottom line is that the source of feeling anxious about presenting is self-consciousness. It may come from evaluating ourselves in relation to a mental picture we've constructed of perfection. Let's put that one to rest right away.

There's no such thing as the perfect presentation. It's one of the wonderful aspects of presenting. You needn't concern yourself with presenting according to some model of perfection because there is no such thing. From one presentation to another, the dynamics constantly change. Even with the same subject—the setting, the people in the audience, the time slot you have on the agenda—everything differs from one occurrence to the next. So presentations flex and change. If they flex and change, there's no way they'll ever fit one preconceived notion of "perfect."

Perhaps more than any other task you undertake, presenting allows for a great deal of latitude. A number of generic topics are being presented these days in meetings, seminars, and training sessions: stress management, time management, excellence, leadership, to name a few. On any given weekday in this country, you can probably find hundreds of presentations and hundreds of presenters speaking on those subjects. Which one is "perfect"?

Yes, there are good presentations and there are bad ones. There are dynamite presenters and dull ones. But since you've come this far in this book, you've already discovered some ways to become a dynamite presenter who has the tools to create a very good presentation.

Being self-conscious about presenting also occurs when we compare ourselves to some criteria we've been led to believe are superior. (Not necessarily "perfect." We've already dispensed with that. Just "better.") If we've heard negative remarks along the way, derogatory or demeaning comments from a significant influence in our lives, we may worry that we won't measure up. That compounds our feelings of anxiousness.

Internalizing these external critics sets off a vicious cycle. You end up being your own worst critic...which heightens your anxiety...which undermines your ability to present...so you criticize yourself even more...which heightens your anxiety even more the next time around. How many times have you come down on yourself for something no one else even noticed? Or if they did, it wasn't really that important? (You forgot to cover a point on your outline. So what?) If this scenario sounds familiar, you've got to break that cycle in order to overcome your anxiousness. Apply these techniques, and get the training and coaching and encouragement that will stop that "nagging critic" in its tracks.

You can begin by acknowledging that your self-criticism is probably unfounded or highly exaggerated. Chances are you make a far better impression than you're giving yourself credit for. I observe this all the time when I coach presenters. Many people assume the worst until they actually see the results.

I videotape a person's presentation, and then we review the tape together. Almost without exception, people are surprised and pleased. They sit back, smiling, and say, "Gee, I didn't think my presentation would look that good!" or "Hey, I did better than I thought!" If that's any indication, you're already presenting better than you think. Which leads us to a second stage: Rethink the way you think about yourself.

Affirm Yourself

One approach to overcoming self-conscious anxiety is to develop a more affirmative view of yourself: a view that's more in line with the facts and less concerned with erroneous perceptions.

There's an old saying, "Accentuate the positive, eliminate the negative." Accentuate what you know to be true of you. Accentuate the value of what's important to you. And eliminate that negative input from others and from yourself.

The story I related earlier about B. provides a perfect example. What B. knew to be true was that she knew her subject like the back of her hand. She was articulate, sincere, and creative. She accentuated those attributes and focused on the value of doing something that was important to her. Her anxiousness about possibly stumbling over her words paled by comparison. She valued making a difference on behalf of her son more than she valued what an external audience might think of her. (As it turned out, they thought very highly of her!)

Our minds function much like a computer. What comes out of the system is based on what's gone into it and how the input's been processed. I observed the effects of this principle when I presented to a group of employees who were being "outplaced" (a nice euphemism for "fired"). If there's ever a time when people need to feel good about themselves, it's when they're out looking for a job.

Midway through my presentation, "Marketing Yourself," one of the women expressed a concern. While she understood the point I was making, she said she felt at a disadvantage because she was overweight. I asked her to take out a clean sheet of paper, write her name across the top, and make a list of what people observed about her. I started by observing, "J., you have excellent posture, which gives you an air of poise and confidence." Someone from across the room added: "J., you have a wonderful smile. It lights up a room!" Then, the woman sitting next to her chimed in, "You're so helpful." And another offered, "You do the job better than anyone else around here." J. walked out of that session with a bounce in her step, a smile on her face, and four self-affirming statements. She'd received the benefit of some very encouraging input.

If you're one of those people who plays the role of Siskel and Ebert and you insist on critiquing yourself, I suggest you take an affirmative approach. Refrain from repeating the things you think you're not, or you don't, or you can't. (That will just fuel your feelings of self-consciousness.)

Instead, affirm what you are, what you do, what you can. Identify your attributes and focus on the "facts" of what you have to bring to an audience. Here are some examples related to presenting that have come from people I've worked with:

I am intelligent.

I have a good sense of humor.

I have a good vocabulary.

I am a caring person.

I am creative.

I am enthusiastic.

I can speak well.

I have ability!

Take a few minutes, right now, to write out at least three self-affirming statements. Say them aloud and repeat them to yourself. And repeat them again whenever you're getting ready to present. Remember: If you want to feel positive about presenting (or anything else for that matter), you need to give yourself positive "inputs" and process them in positive ways.

Apply a Relaxation Technique

Much research has been done on human behavior, and one group has specifically addressed *call reluctance,* the hesitation or anxiety some people feel when they have to initiate contact with others. In their book, *The Psychology of Call Reluctance: How to Overcome the Fear of Self-Promotion,* authors Dudley and Goodson have identified and described several forms of call reluctance. Not surprisingly, one form is anxiety about speaking before groups.

Their research indicates that anxiety about speaking before groups:

> ...appears to be entirely learned. It may come from inexperience as a group speaker or from an early traumatic experience giving a group presentation. Group call reluctance is among the easiest to correct when it is properly assessed and the proper training supports are used."[1]

Dudley and Goodson offer several prescriptions for overcoming group anxiety. One such prescription is what they term "sensory injection." (Not being a psychologist, I call it "stop and smell the roses.") With this technique, you train yourself to relax in response to a cue. It's an easy procedure to follow, and it works.

Here's what you do. First, select a recording that you find pleasing and relaxing. Soothing music, a poetry reading, or a relaxation-training tape will do. Next, select a fragrance that's pleasing to you. It should be a scent you don't use or associate with someone or something else. Put a dab of that fragrance on a cotton ball. Now, you're ready to apply the technique.

1. Sit or lie down in a comfortable position.

2. Listen to the recording and relax. (Breathe slowly and deeply.)

3. When you feel relaxed, inhale the fragrance from the cotton ball for one to three minutes.

4. Repeat the process four or five times.

The effect of this "prescription" is that you come to associate the fragrance with the feeling of being relaxed. Whenever you inhale that fragrance, it will elicit a positive relaxation response.

Obviously, when you're relaxed, you're not nervous. So, if you start to feel nervous before a presentation, stop and smell the roses! Take a moment to whiff the fragrance that causes you to relax. (If you feel silly sniffing a cotton ball, use a handkerchief instead.)

Repetition reinforces. If this technique doesn't work one hundred percent the very first time you try it, don't give up. Repeat it. Try it the next time you present. You'll relax a bit. Use it again the second time you present. You'll feel more relaxed. By the time you get around to your third or fourth presentation, you'll find you're completely (or almost completely) relaxed and feelin' good about yourself.

Supporters

I was recently asked how I handle a difficult group. I hadn't really thought about it before. As I did think about it (in order to answer the question), I realized I don't view groups as "difficult" or "easy." Oh, there may be one or two people in a group who could be described as "difficult." Anyone who presents enough will eventually run into those. But I don't take them personally or too seriously.

What I do take personally are supporters. And I make a point of gathering support before I present. Like a politician on a campaign trail, you want to know who you can count on. You want to know who you can look to for encouragement.

Having supporters in an audience makes a group "easy." It also makes your experience of presenting more pleasant. That's important. After a couple of pleasant experiences presenting, you'll look forward (without anxiety) to additional opportunities to present.

How do you gather support? You make a point of getting to know at least one or two people who are advocates. You begin to form affirmative relationships before your presentation even begins.

If you're presenting in a familiar situation, such as addressing a group in your workplace, preview some points of your presentation with one or two of your peers. By doing so, you identify in advance who your supporters are, who is likely to agree with your position. They may offer one or two suggestions or additional insights. If you incorporate these in your presentation (giving credit, of course, where credit is due), you really have an advocate.

When you present and deliver this point or that, you'll spot your supporters smiling with approval. You'll see a head nodding yes in agreement. You'll be encouraged by people in the audience who signal acceptance—of you and your message. It's what we all want when we're up in front of a group: approval, agreement, acceptance. The big A's that affirm us.

When you present in a new situation, such as addressing a group at an outside event, make a point of getting to know at least one or two people who will be in the audience. You'll probably already have a contact: the person who invited you to speak or the emcee. But you also want to get to know some of the "regular folks" who will be out there.

Arrive early enough to meet some people personally. Have a cup of coffee with them and some pleasant conversation. Doing so puts faces and names on an otherwise impersonal body of strangers. You'll find you feel more at home when you can relate to an audience on a more personal basis. You may have met only one Jack or Jane beforehand, but the audience is full of Jacks and Janes. Nice folks, looking forward to your speech, upon whom you can look as supporters.

Groups don't need to be difficult. In fact, they're usually wonderful to deal with. For every one detractor in an audience, you'll find you have fifty or a hundred potential supporters. Most people want the presenter to do well. When you do, it's a better experience for them.

The Value of Being Prepared

There's nothing that will better prepare you for doing well when you present than being well prepared. People who feel assured of doing well are rarely anxious.

Imagine how anxious an infantryman would feel being sent into battle without a weapon. Imagine how anxious a tennis player would feel entering a competition match without ever having had a lesson before. Ridiculous? Try this one. Imagine how anxious a person would feel getting up before a group without having had training or practice in presenting.

We don't expect salespeople to sell without benefit of sales training. We don't expect managers to excel without benefit of management training or experience. We don't expect athletes to win without benefit of coaching and practice. But we do expect that people should be able to present—off the cuff. That doesn't make any sense.

I've witnessed, again and again, the value of training, preparation, and practice in a course I teach on presentations. The participants deliver four presentations, all of them on the same subject. The first is graded only on organization; the second only on relational skills; the third on delivery, with audiovisuals; and the fourth and final one on everything. What happens between the first and final presentations is wonderful to behold. By the end of the course, people are relaxed, enthused, expressive. They've gained such familiarity with their subject and with the feeling of being on stage that they step up in front of the group with confidence. In just a few sessions, people who were breathless with anxiety, whose hands shook with nervousness, are addressing a group with ease.

You can address a group with ease, provided you're well prepared. Start by getting training in presenting. Once you've gained the insights, skills, and techniques for delivering an effective presentation, prepare one. Not the night before. Prepare well enough in advance so you have the time to practice your material. The better prepared you are, the less anxious you'll be.

In Perspective

Anxiety about presenting can be overcome when we put it in proper perspective. It's not a dreadful fear of public speaking. It's a common case of nervousness. We acknowledge there's no logical reason to feel anxious. We're just self-conscious.

Slip your hand into your pocket. Ah, there's your one hundred dollar "a-bill-ity." Take a whiff of that scented cotton ball. Ah, now you're relaxed. If you're not laughing by now (that's the best prescription for anxiety), spot one of your supporters and repeat your self-affirmations.

Imagine the day when you calmly and confidently step up to the front of a group. You've overcome your anxieties. The jitters you feel are minimal and you've got them under control. You skillfully deliver a well-prepared presentation! You have now joined the ranks of those who distinguish themselves from the crowd, of those who have the potential to make a difference. When you put these suggestions into practice, that day could be tomorrow!

To Overcome Anxiety Like a Pro, Remember

- It's not fear. It's nervousness.
- Acknowledge the source: self-consciousness.
- Recognize the solution: your ability.
- Think affirmatively: "I am...I can...I have..."

- Stop and smell the roses: relax.
- Gather support in advance.

Reference

1. Goerge W. Dudley and Shannon L. Goodson, *The Psychology of Call Reluctance: How to Overcome the Fear of Self-Promotion,* Behavioral Science Research Press, Dallas, 1986, p. 52.

7
Dealing With Difficulties, or Mastering the "Uns"

Your material is in hand, your skills are well honed, and your anxiety about speaking before groups is under control. You've heard about the pitfalls that can beset a presentation. But you're not one to be caught off guard (especially in front of a group). You've done your homework.

By planning ahead you've taken into account all of the factors that can affect your performance. You've profiled the audience and planned your presentation in relation to the people you'll be addressing. You've prepared a well-structured message and practiced it. You've checked out the "mechanics" ahead of time: audiovisuals, equipment, and facilities.

You arrive well in advance of the time you're scheduled to present. You have backups on hand, extras of everything you need. And you know the person who's in charge.

In short, you've done everything possible to eliminate surprises.

It's your turn on the agenda. You're ready. You step to the head of the room, face your audience with confidence, and begin to deliver your message. Then...it happens. The unexpected difficulty.

They strike even the best prepared presenters. They're unpredictable events that can threaten to disrupt a presentation. They fall into three categories that I refer to as the "uns" (because in every case it's *unfor*tunate that it's happening to you). There's the unexpected accident, the unforeseen incident, and the undesirable behavior.

You'll be able to deal with disaster when you learn to master the "uns." How you do so depends on which type you're confronted with at the time.

The Unexpected Accident

A long-time business associate invited me to present to a group that was very important to him. I knew he was counting on me to do a good job, since how I came across would reflect on him. I was counting on myself to do a good job, since he's a special client and a good friend. The pressure was on.

Twenty minutes before the group was due to arrive, I noticed that the front of my jacket was stained with a streak of black grease. (I'd moved an overhead projector and later discovered there was grease on the cord.) I was wearing a light-colored suit that day, so the mark was very visible.

In this particular situation, advance planning paid off. I had a backup change of clothes in my car. I'd arrived early enough so I had time to make the change. By the time I was called on to present, I was calm, cool, collected—and clean. And the audience was none the wiser.

Recovering from the unexpected accident is not always so easily done. Some accidents are so unexpected that no amount of planning can prepare you for them. You just have to handle them as they occur. As did one presenter who dealt with a difficult situation with aplomb.

A woman who is a highly admired author of Christian books was the featured speaker at one of Billy Graham's crusades. The master of ceremonies gave her a glowing introduction to an audience that numbered in the thousands. She rose from her seat and started to walk up the steps that led to the speakers' platform. Half way up, the heel of her shoe caught in the hem of her full-length formal dress. She stumbled and fell, splat, right on her face. A hush fell over the crowd.

Billy Graham rushed over. He took hold of her arm to help her to her feet, but the heel had become entangled in the hem. She tripped again. After what must have seemed an eternity to her (although it was really only a matter of seconds), she finally made it up on her feet. She walked gracefully to the podium and looked steadily out at the audience. In a tone of mock seriousness she said: "Well, now all of you know the truth. I've fallen for Billy Graham." The audience roared with laughter. Her presentation was a great success.

In a situation some presenters would consider the ultimate embarrassment, this presenter regained her composure. She put the audience at ease using a wonderful technique: humor.

It's interesting to note that the words *humor* and *human* are closely related. We humans, ever subject to error and accidents, can usually handle them best with humor. Laughter really is good medicine. A healthy dose of humor relieves tension for both you and your audience.

Humor will endear you to people, provided it's good-natured humor. That doesn't mean going into a presentation armed with an arsenal of jokes. It doesn't mean serving up black humor, which is sarcastic or sadistic in intent. It means reacting with a light-hearted response. It's finding an aspect that's funny about an otherwise "unfunny" situation.

When I reflect on the quality of humor, I'm reminded of a time I boarded a crowded commuter flight. As I was walking down the aisle to my seat, a hanger sticking out of the top of the garment bag I was carrying caught on the seatbelt of another passenger. I stopped abruptly in my tracks, feeling self-conscious about holding up traffic in the aisle and being stuck on this passenger's seat. (Those were the days when I took just about everything seriously.) I looked down at the gentleman, apologized, and said, "I think I'm hung up on you." He loosened the hanger, smiled, and answered, "Gosh, I'm awfully sorry, I'm a happily married man." That's humor. (That's a person who would make a good presenter.)

On another occasion, I was observing presentations given by students in a class I was teaching. One poor soul was having one of those days when nothing was going his way. His papers slid off of the podium. He fumbled the chalkboard eraser and it dusted the front of his suit. The overhead projector bulb burned out midway through his presentation. He tripped on the cord when he walked back across the room.

For people who couldn't see the lighter side, these accidents would have been enough to make them flee the scene. But this young man straightened up, smiled broadly at his audience, and said, "What you're seeing here is a live demonstration of Murphy's Law at its worst." He laughed. The audience laughed. And somehow, he related the point to his subject and continued his presentation.

Humor can turn an awkward situation into an enjoyable experience. It's enjoyable for the audience because they laugh, and laughter makes people feel good. It's enjoyable for you as the presenter because it diffuses the tension of a difficult moment. And humor can make a presentation memorable.

I don't remember every point made by the speaker at Billy Graham's crusade, but I will long remember how graciously she recovered from the unexpected. I can't for the life of me remember the subject on which that student spoke, but I will long remember the line he used to make the most of a bad situation. I've even used it a couple of times myself.

If you lack a spontaneous sense of humor, how do you develop one? Three approaches have worked for me and others.

- Keep things in perspective.
- Focus on the audience.
- Look for the amusing.

Keep Things in Perspective

You feel your presentation is important. It is. The subject and the setting may be intense. But in the larger scheme of things, no presentation is a matter of life or death. Contrary to what you might think, the sun does not rise and set on the basis of how well you present. And generally, even the worst situation is not as bad as you imagine. With the proper perspective, you can say, "This is not so terribly serious." In fact, days later you'll probably laugh about it.

Focus on the Audience

Every presentation is intended primarily for the people you're addressing. The interest, energy, and enthusiasm you create are for their benefit. When you care more about their experience and discount the importance of yours, it relieves you of a terrible burden: preoccupation with perfection.

Perfectionism is really a self-centered trait that often results in the very opposite of what it aims to achieve. For example, procrastination is frequently associated with perfectionism. The procrastinator puts off doing something for fear it won't be perfect and consequently doesn't get around to doing it at all. The perfectionist speaker is preoccupied with delivering a flawless presentation and consequently loses sight of the humor (and the human) that's inherent in every flaw. Presenters who demand perfection of themselves can find disaster even in minor mishaps.

People who present like pros aren't concerned with being perfect. They are concerned with being prepared. Very well prepared. When you're well prepared you can more easily relax and focus attention on the people in your audience. When you're well prepared and relaxed, you convey more confidence. Confident presenters can make a light-hearted, humorous response without putting the seriousness of the subject at risk. One factor (preparedness) contributes to the other (confidence). Together, they put you at ease and open your eyes to what's humorous in a difficult situation.

When you focus on the audience you also recognize that when something goes awry, it isn't happening just to you. It's happening to everyone in the room. As a pro, you want to relieve the awkward moment for the benefit of your listeners. When you focus on the audience rather than on yourself, you recognize, "This isn't personal."

Look for the Amusing

Seeing the humor in a situation comes more easily and naturally if you're receptive to it. Every difficulty is like a two-sided coin. On the one side is the dread that it detracts from your VIP (very important presentation). It's likely it will if you view it that way and take the unexpected seriously and personally.

The other side of the coin is an opportunity to use the unexpected to contribute to your presentation. When you find something amusing in the unexpected, you can acknowledge, "This isn't threatening." You can take what happened and turn it to your advantage. You can accentuate a point of content by handling the point with humor.

Perhaps more important, you can enhance how you're perceived by people by showing yourself to be human. It's a principle I was alerted to some years ago while I was in training as a new employee with IBM. There I was, a rookie, and I had to deliver a presentation to a manager I held in some awe. I practiced and practiced for days until I had it down to perfection.

After I delivered the presentation, the manager called me into his office and asked me to do it over again the next day. When I asked him what I'd done wrong, he said, "Nothing. And that's the problem. People won't think you're human."

Since then I've had numerous opportunities to deal with the unexpected, and numerous occasions when I've shown I'm all too human (i.e., flawed). I've come to appreciate the value of that manager's advice.

Don't take yourself too seriously, don't take the incident personally, and don't view an error or an accident as a threat. With humor even the worst that you can imagine can be transformed into a moment that will make you, and your audience, laugh. When that happens, you've mastered the unexpected.

The Unforeseen Incident

There is a corollary to Murphy's Law: "If something can go wrong, it will." It's the Presenter's Premise: "If there's one thing you can foresee, it's that the unforeseen will occur." Not always. But often enough to make you realize that all your advance planning and preparation won't account for every eventuality.

Like many presenters, I've encountered difficulty in the form of the unforeseen incident. The sound system goes on the blink. Someone in the audience collapses from a heart attack. Workbooks shipped well in advance of the date of a presentation are mysteriously lost in transit. An earthquake shakes the building. Lights go out because of a power failure. (I'm not making these incidents up. They've actually happened to me, and probably to more than a few other presenters as well.) I imagine a group of people who have presented could compile a pretty humorous book based on the unforeseen incidents they've had to contend with.

So how do you contend with them? As with the unexpected accident, humor may be one way. However, there are occasions when a humorous response obviously isn't appropriate. Heart attacks and earthquakes are not laughing matters. If not humor, then what?

As the presenter, you're in the best position to determine what specific response to make. What you do will naturally depend on the nature and extent of the incident. But, in general, you want to demonstrate leadership. You're the person on the platform commanding the attention of the audience. (At least you are if you're presenting like a pro.) Throughout your presentation, the audience, whether it's one person or a thousand, is looking at you. That means they're also looking to you for cues. "What's going to happen now?" is the thought that runs through their minds. They expect you to know how to deal with incidents that occur when you're at the head of the room.

I have a cousin who's an avid sailor. He feels about sailing as I do about presenting: he works at it to give it his very best. His heart is in it, and when he races he sails his boat to win. But there are times when the wind isn't favorable and he has to take a different tack. He has to change course or direction in order to advance.

Presenting is much the same. When an unforeseen incident takes the wind out of your sails, you may have to take a different tack. When this kind of difficulty occurs, quickly recall these three points.

- Don't get flustered.
- Figure out the next best step.
- Be flexible.

Don't Get Flustered

Remain calm and composed. Remember the power of perception? If you're perceived as someone who falls apart when the least little upset occurs, it will undermine your credibility. Your stomach may be tied into knots on the inside, but you should concentrate on maintaining at least an outward appearance of composure. When you do, it's surprising how well faking it works. You actually do become more composed.

More important, it's harder to think clearly when you're flustered. When you can calmly assess the situation, you're better equipped to determine what tack to take next.

Figure Out the Next Best Step

After my sister obtained her pilot's license, she continued taking flying lessons to obtain an instrument rating. On one flight her instructor took her to the San Francisco Bay Area where the air traffic is particularly heavy. To test her aptitude using only instruments, her head and the instrument panel were covered with a hood. The navigation chart was open on her lap, and she had a flashlight in hand to illuminate the chart.

Suddenly, an air traffic controller's voice came over the radio requesting her aircraft identification. Without thinking, she raised the flashlight to her mouth and pronounced her call letters. The controller radioed the request again. Flustered, she raised the flashlight to her mouth again, and this time shouted her call letters. When the traffic controller demanded the airplane identification a third time, the flight instructor took over.

Later, when they were back down on the ground, the flight instructor interrupted the verbal flogging she was giving herself. "You can't change what happened," he told her. "Just get on with the next best thing." The principle applies to presenters as well as pilots.

When the unforeseen incident happens, get on with the next best thing. Figure out what needs to be done under the circumstances, and do it. Either detour, delay, or dismiss.

Let's consider how each option applies to the same situation. Suppose you are presenting to a large audience in an auditorium setting that requires a sound system for the speaker to be heard. You're introduced, you step to the podium, you begin your presentation. And within minutes, the sound system fails. There's no way you can go on without it functioning. People can't hear you past the third row. What do you do?

Here's how one presenter handled this disaster, and the tactics he employed. He was speaking on the subject of employee management to a group of supervisors, managers, and business owners, although the same techniques could be applied with just about any topic. He knew a sound technician was on hand and was aware of the problem. What he didn't know was how long it would take to be fixed.

Detour When you detour, you take another route to reach your ultimate destination. The objective of your presentation can still be achieved. You just have to go about it another way. In this case the presenter knew he couldn't be heard. But he could be seen. So he took that tack. On a transparency projected on a large overhead screen, he wrote in bold letters:

> WRITE OUT THREE PROBLEMS
> YOU'VE HAD
> MANAGING EMPLOYEES

That bought him some time, but it wasn't enough. The sound system still wasn't working. So he wrote on a second transparency:

> TALK WITH THE PERSON
> ON YOUR LEFT
> ABOUT IT

All the while, he kept his sense of humor. When he stepped to the overhead projector to write his instructions, he smiled broadly and added sweeping gestures. He kept the audience at ease and laughing the whole time.

Delay Several minutes had gone by and the sound system still wasn't fixed. He'd detoured about as long as he could. When he observed that the audience was growing restless, he stepped to the overhead projector for a third time, and wrote:

> LET'S TAKE A
> 15-MINUTE BREAK!

When in doubt, stall.

He knew the technician was working on the system, and there was nothing further he could do. He made a point of going out into the lobby where he joined the crowd. He introduced himself, shook hands, and mingled among the group. He made himself accessible to people, and he made light of the situation. If he wasn't distressed by the unforeseen, the audience would be less likely to be.

Dismiss   You can delay people for a fifteen-minute coffee break, but not for the three hours it was estimated it would take to repair the system. He dismissed the group. It's a last resort, but sometimes it's the next best thing to do.

After the audience had filed back into the auditorium, the presenter wrote a fourth and final message:

SORRY

STILL NO SOUND

#!@#!

WE'LL RECONVENE

AT 1:30 P.M.

THANK YOU

Although this was an extreme incident, it serves to illustrate the three tactics you can apply in any unforeseen circumstance: detour, delay, or dismiss.

What do you do if the materials you usually use aren't on hand? Detour. What do you do if someone in the audience collapses? Delay. What do you do if an earthquake or other natural disaster strikes in the middle of your presentation? Dismiss. (Chances are the audience will dismiss themselves!) With every such incident, one or a combination of these tactics will work.

With some unforeseen incidents, you can use a catch phrase to bridge the gap between the smooth, planned portions of your presentation and the moment when disaster strikes. One such phrase that comes in handy is, "I'm glad that happened. It gives me a chance to..."

When attending a product announcement presentation, I saw a presenter use this technique with ease. She was presenting a seminar on a new computer system. The system was turned on, loaded, and ready to run. She took a few minutes to address the group, then turned toward the system to demonstrate some of its functions. At a critical point in her demonstration, the screen went blank, the lights went out, and there was silence. A power failure.

She reacted with calm, good-natured humor. "If any of you were feeling in the dark about this new system, take heart. Now, we're all in the dark." Soon after she finished speaking, the power was restored, and the lights came back on. Of course, the computer screen was still blank.

"I'm glad that happened," she said. "It gives me a chance to demonstrate how easy it is to restart the system in the event a power failure happens in your offices." She resumed her presentation.

This presenter used all the right techniques for dealing with the unforeseen. She didn't get flustered. She figured out the next best step. And she was flexible. She couldn't just continue from the point where she had left off. She had to adapt her presentation to the circumstances.

Be Flexible

That unforeseen incidents happen is one of the best reasons for being well prepared. The more you present and plan and prepare, the more you minimize the unforeseen. After a while, there just isn't much you haven't seen and handled before. But when the unforeseen does occur, you're better equipped to adapt when you're very well prepared and when you really know your subject. It's one of the best reasons for not relying on a memorized script. The unforeseen demands flexibility.

The importance of being flexible is illustrated by these examples of difficulties that are common occurrences for presenters.

What would you do if...? You're invited to be the guest speaker at the next luncheon meeting of a professional association. You confirm your time frame in advance with the program director. You go into the meeting having been told you'll have fifteen minutes to speak. That's what you've prepared for. Just before you go on, the program director leans over and whispers in your ear, "There's been a change in the agenda." At the last minute you learn you're expected to speak for thirty minutes, or you're only allowed ten. It happens. You have to be flexible.

Do a quick mental review of your key points and supporting material. Determine what you can condense or eliminate if you need to deliver your message in less time or what you can expand if you have more time to fill. In either case, always honor the time frame you've been given, even if it's been changed at the last moment.

What would you do if...? You arrive to deliver a presentation to an audience you've been told will number about twenty-five. In the meantime, an emergency has come up. Four people show. Or, the word has gotten out, other departments have been asked to attend, and a hundred people show up. It happens. You have to be flexible.

In this case, adapt your style. A smaller group will respond best to a more interactive setting; a larger group to a proactive one. In a smaller group, find out people's names and use them. For a larger group, find out who's represented (by department, for example) so you can incorporate references to various areas of interest. In either case, present to the group as though it's exactly the size audience you expected. Whether one person is present or one hundred, you want to affirm them.

What would you do if...? You open the morning newspaper and find the company you work for is featured on the front page. They're involved in a matter that affects the community, and your department is on the "front lines." Moments later, a senior executive calls and asks you to make a presentation at a public meeting that afternoon.

The principles and techniques of presenting don't vary because a presentation is a response to a crisis. If anything, they become more important as a means of demonstrating articulate leadership. In a crisis situation, pay attention to three factors in particular.

First, remember the power of perceptions. The facts of the matter may, in fact, be in your favor. Your challenge is to create perceptions that are, too. Second, the relational elements of presenting (covered in Chapter 3) are especially important. People in crisis will resent being preached at. They need to be nurtured: told what they can expect, reassured they're recognized, drawn into your message, and given an understanding of how what you're saying applies to them. Finally, tap into your resources. You can produce a faster and better response when you make use of available talent and tools: administrative staff to gather background material, confirm the facts, prepare visual aids, and provide input you may find useful and creative.

Flexibility is a great asset in a presenter. It will earn you high marks with the people who invite you to speak, because it reflects your willingness to accommodate their agendas. It will earn you high marks with audiences who listen to you, because they'll never suspect anything is amiss. And it serves you well when you need to react quickly to the occasional unforeseen incident.

The Undesirable Behavior

I've encountered many disasters when presenting: earthquake tremors, a tornado, and numerous power failures, to name just a few. Such natural disasters don't hold a candle to the person in the audience who's behaving in an undesirable way. There's nothing that has more potential to disrupt a presentation than someone who repeatedly interrupts, objects, contradicts, jokes around, and the like. They're detractors in that their behavior threatens to detract from the quality of your presentation.

Detractors interrupt the flow of a presentation. They have a negative effect on the otherwise affirmative climate you're trying to create. They can diminish the value others might receive if you were allowed to proceed without disruption. For the benefit of the audience as a whole, you need to deal with the one or two who behave in an undesirable way.

You can spot them from the edge of a conference room table or from a podium a mile away. Some detractors wear a facial expression that signals they're ready to pick a fight. Some sit hunched in their chairs, shoulders slouched, arms crossed tightly together. Others sit upright with their heads slightly cocked, a wry smirk giving them away. Still others look so stony-faced and rigid you want to reach over and check if they have a pulse.

Regardless of the posture or expression they may bring to a presentation, they're the people who are waiting for an opportunity to pounce. They're at your presentation not to hear, but to be heard. And they'll vocalize whenever there's an opening.

For that reason, detractors appear most often (or at least they're most noticeable) in small to medium-sized interactive groups and in mandated settings. The boss asked them to attend the meeting or seminar. The company's conducting the training session for the whole department. For obvious reasons, they're less evident in larger convention-style audiences and in exclusively proactive settings.

Reasons

What leads people to disrupt a presentation? I've observed three reasons. When you can identify (and sometimes even empathize with) what motivates a person to behave badly, you'll be better able to deal with these difficult personalities.

Resistance to Change Presentations often serve the purpose of delivering information or ideas that are new or that challenge people's thinking. Some people aren't receptive to new ideas. They're unwilling to entertain attitudes or actions that differ from ones they've harbored for a long time.

In such cases, disrupting a presentation is a form of self-defense. It's a means of counteracting ideas and information people just can't bring themselves to hear.

I suppose their logic works something along these lines. "If I ask a question he can't answer, then this information is no good." "If I raise an objection she can't dispel, then this program is a bunch of hogwash." In effect, if the person succeeds in disrupting your presentation, they've satisfied themselves that you have no credibility and they can continue to cling to their old, comfortable ways.

Resentment About Your Role Standing at the head of the room presenting, you're in a leadership role. During the time you're delivering your ten-minute speech or conducting the week's training session, you're leading the audience through your material and managing the people in the group.

There are those who resent what they perceive to be an intrusion on your part. If you're an outsider (a consultant, contract trainer, guest speaker), they resent your assuming leadership in their territory, so to speak. If you're from within the organization (a subordinate, coworker, sometimes even the manager), they resent your exercising authority over them.

That may, in fact, not be your intent. You may be up there just doing your job. But we've already seen how perception is more powerful than fact. There are people who take offense at leadership when they perceive it impinges on them.

Repeating "Successful" Behavior   People do what has worked for them in the past. When they get what they want by acting in a certain way, they'll act that way again to get what they want. What does the detractor in the audience want? The same thing every one of us wants: attention.

The parent pays attention to the child who throws a temper tantrum. It's successful. The child gets what he or she wants. So what do they do the next time they want attention? They throw a temper tantrum.

Presenters pay attention to people in the audience who disrupt: people who repeatedly vocalize objections, who ask outlandish questions, who ridicule or play the rude jester. So what do they do the next time they want attention? They disrupt your presentation.

At the heart of every one of these factors is a need. That's where your relational skills come in. People need to be affirmed. They need to be recognized. They need to be encouraged and enthused. People in an audience who exhibit undesirable behavior just have a greater need than others and more unappealing ways of showing it. When we understand the source of their behavior, we can detach ourselves from taking their actions personally.

Most of us aren't partial to sarcastic remarks, especially when they're aimed at us. We much prefer dealing with the person who agrees with us than with someone who raises objections or asks questions we can't answer. Nonetheless, if we can recognize that such behavior isn't a personal attack but a means of acting out a need for attention, we can more readily deal with it with trained and practiced skill. Reacting emotionally out of a sense of personal rejection won't solve the problem.

Responses

How do you deal with detractors? For starters, employ the relational techniques described in Chapter 3. By doing so, you'll satisfy most people's needs so that they'll sit back, relax, and attend to your presentation. However, there may still be one or two in the audience who just can't get enough: enough affirmation, enough recognition, enough of a chance to participate and to make themselves heard. When that's the case, try the following approaches.

- Be courteous.
- Exercise control.
- Confront.

Be Courteous   There's a familiar adage that suggests, "You can catch more flies with honey than with vinegar." When it comes to dealing with people, honey equates to common courtesy. Respond to a detractor with the same courtesy you would offer the most agreeable person in the group. Courtesy is expressed by more than words alone. It shows in what you do. It shows in your posture, your facial expression, your tone of voice, as well as in how you verbalize your response.

Picture what a person looks like when they're expressing frustration, aggravation, or impatience. That's exactly the kind of reaction that a detractor is trying to provoke from you. And it's exactly what you don't want to do. If they know they've succeeded in "getting your goat," chances are they'll repeat the behavior. It won't be long before they've gained the upper hand, and you'll have lost your credibility as the presenter.

There are people who disrupt a presentation in a manner that puts your inclination to be courteous to the test. I remember one such gentleman (I use the term lightly) from an experience early in my career. I was asked to deliver a presentation to a group of business education teachers. Since a conference room wasn't available at the school site, we met in one of the classrooms. As soon as I began speaking, this gentleman seated in the back of the room turned on an electric typewriter. He pressed the space bar.

If you've ever used an old electric typewriter, you know the sound that creates. I stopped speaking. He stopped pressing. I started speaking. He started pressing.

Then I looked him squarely in the face and said, courteously but confidently, "Excuse me, sir. For the benefit of everyone else here, I'd appreciate it if you'd please turn off the typewriter. Thank you."

A courteous response will, it is hoped, accomplish two things. You give the person the positive recognition that satisfies their need, and your graciousness appeals to some kindly streak in them. Notice I said "it is hoped." Courtesy isn't always enough. When a detractor persists in being disruptive, follow the steps outlined earlier. Don't get flustered, and figure out the next best step. In the case of undesirable behavior, the next best step is to exercise control.

Control Affirming people with a courteous response doesn't always suffice to put their disruptive behavior to rest. You may have to intensify the way you handle it and advance from "affirmative" to "assertive." In other words, take the initiative and demonstrate that you're in control of the situation.

In the case of the gentleman with the space bar, being courteous didn't have the desired effect. He repeated his disruptive behavior. I knew I had the audience on my side. You usually do in such situations. Their expressions told me they were more annoyed with him than I was. Without saying a word, I walked to the back of the room, unplugged the machine, picked it up off the desk and moved it away. You're better off risking the disfavor of one person than the tens or hundreds of others in the group.

Maintaining control of the environment is one of your responsibilities as a presenter. To give your audience a meaningful and memorable experience, you need to manage the setting in which that experience occurs. You're a kind of traffic cop, monitoring the actions and interactions of people within the group. Sometimes you have to exert control.

What do you say to the detractor who repeatedly questions or objects? Responses like these make the point that you're in control:

"I appreciate your interest in this subject, but in the interest of time, I'm going to have to ask you to hold your questions. I'll be happy to discuss them with you at the break, or when the session is over." Then you proceed with your presentation.

"We have time for just one more comment before we go on." Then recognize someone else in the group.

"If you have questions or comments, please make note of them as we go along. We'll take time to discuss them at the end of the session." If your message, the setting, or your personal preference call for an uninterrupted presentation, let your listeners know at the outset that they'll have a chance to speak at the end.

Especially when I present to smaller groups, I prefer creating an interactive setting. People gain more when they have a chance to participate. It makes a presentation more meaningful and memorable for them. However, when your time frame is limited, you need to maintain tighter control. When you observe detractors in the audience, you'll want to maintain tighter control. And when you present in more formal settings, you're expected to maintain control. Those are times when you want to make a point of deferring questions until your presentation is over.

Knowing how to field questions and handle objections effectively is a common concern for presenters, especially for those who present in interactive settings. In order to do the subject justice, it's treated separately in the next chapter.

Confront   When a person persists in being disruptive (the more accurate word may be obnoxious), you have the audience as a whole to consider. The experience of the many takes precedence over the one or two. When courtesy and control fail to solve the problem, your last resort is to confront the detractor.

If possible, announce a short coffee break. That gives you the opportunity to call the person aside so you can deal with them privately. In that way, you avoid embarrassing them. You also avoid being drawn into a public battle of wits, which you just might lose.

When you confront the person, do so with both courtesy and control. With a confident posture and steady tone of voice, maintaining eye contact with the person, firmly say something like this: "For the benefit of the group, I'm going to have to ask that you refrain from [specify the undesirable behavior] until this meeting is over." For example, "For the benefit of the group, I'm going to have to ask that you refrain from chatting with the person seated next to you until this meeting is over."

Phrases like "for the benefit of the group" and "in the interest of time" take you off the hook. They indicate that you're not confronting them for personal reasons, but because you have the interest of the audience in mind.

Because of the peer pressure that exists in any group, the first two tactics—courtesy and control—usually bring disruptions to a halt. You should rarely have to confront people. But if you do, remember: While you're presenting, you're in charge. It's one of the reasons for developing very good presentations. You can demonstrate your leadership through skill. The more you master presenting, the easier it is to master the "uns."

Unplugging

Imagine there's a person in the audience who's resistant, resentful, or waiting for a chance to gain attention. Think of them as being plugged in to an electrical outlet. If they hear or see something from a presenter they don't like, it's like a surge of power that sets them off.

Some people present in such a manner (albeit perhaps unconsciously) that they invite disruptions from detractors. Be careful not to give the impression that you're preaching at or talking down to people. Watch that you don't present material as though yours is the only point of view.

Even when you may do everything right, you still may offend some people, for reasons known only to them. You present with confidence and someone in the audience perceives that it's conceit. You emphasize a point and someone in the audience sets out to prove you wrong. You may be able to dispel these kinds of misperceptions and avoid disruptions altogether by using a technique referred to as "unplugging." Unplugging offers your listeners an affirmation that pulls the plug on potentially negative reactions.

Statements like these are intended to "unplug" potential detractors:

"I know everyone won't agree with all the material I'll be presenting, but I hope you'll find something of value that will make it worth your while."

"This is just one of many programs on the subject, but it's one that's worked for many people."

There are two schools of thought on unplugging. Some presenters prefer to do it at the outset of a presentation, to set the record straight right up front. Others prefer to wait until they observe that there may be a need to unplug.

I prefer to wait. An effective presentation begins with an opener that captures the audience's attention. There's nothing attention-getting about an unplugging statement. Moreover, you may not need to unplug. If you're an enthused and caring presenter using all the right relational skills, potential detractors may let down their guard naturally.

In any case, if you're observing people's reactions (the signals they send) as you should be, you can determine the mood of your listeners early on. If the group is wholly receptive, you don't need to unplug. If a majority of the group is resistant, you're going to have to work a whole lot harder at breaking them down than uttering a simple statement. It's when one or two appear to be potential detractors that unplugging can be most useful. Then, relate the statement after your preview, before you get into the body of your presentation. Detractors don't usually interrupt before then anyway.

When You're in the Audience

As a presenter, you understand how difficult it can be to deal with detractors. Don't be one yourself when you're a member of the audience. Be kind to your fellow presenters.

The Next Best Thing

If there's one experience all presenters share in common it's having to deal with difficulties. At some time in the course of your career, you're going to confront the "uns": unexpected accidents, unforeseen incidents, and undesirable behavior from one of your listeners. In that respect, presenting is a slice of life. The unplanned just has a way of happening. It's one of the things that makes presenting challenging.

When you encounter a difficult situation, bear two things in mind. First, recall the techniques we've covered in this chapter. Second, recall what other professionals do. They pick themselves up and go on.

Actors ad-lib when they forget their lines. Athletes recover from falls and continue as if nothing happened. Entertainers make blunders, but the show goes on. In every field of endeavor the real pros are those who excel not just when all of the conditions are right, but most especially when something goes wrong.

In a best-case, worst-case scenario: The best that can happen is that you'll deal with the difficulty in such a way that no one suspects anything's wrong. The worst that can happen is that the audience will see you're human. And that could be the best thing that can happen.

To Deal With Difficulties Like a Pro, Remember

- Prior planning prevents poor presentations.

The Unexpected Accident	Keep things in perspective.
	Focus on the audience.
	Look for the amusing.
The Unforeseen Incident	Don't get flustered.
	Figure out the next best step: detour... delay...dismiss.
	Be flexible.
The Undesirable Behavior	Understand their reasons:
	Resistance to change
	Role resentment
	Repeating behaviors that get attention
	Use these responses:
	Be courteous.
	Exercise control.
	Confront.

- Be kind to your fellow presenters.

8

Fielding Questions and Comments

You're playing center field. A member of the opposing team steps up to bat, whacks the ball and sends a pop fly in your direction. You're a pro. You can handle it. You catch it neatly, zing it home, and the batter returns to the box. The crowd roars, applauding your obvious skill.

That's the way presenters would like to respond to questions and comments. We'd like to know we can field just about anything someone in the audience might send our way. Whether it's a question we can answer or one we can't, a valid objection or a ludicrous one, we'd like to handle it with ease.

Whenever you're on your feet, you're on the spot. All eyes are focused on you. As long as you're in the speaking mode, you're in the captain's seat. You have control over the presentation.

But as soon as you take questions or comments from the group, there's no telling what will happen. And you don't have much time to think. If you're going to maintain control of your presentation and your credibility with the group, you need to be adept at fielding questions and comments.

Being Prepared

Here again, planning and preparation pay off. How's that? "How can I know ahead of time what people will ask or what comments they'll make?" That's a good question.

From Experience

If you've dealt with the subject of your presentation before, you know from experience some of the concerns that are likely to cross people's minds.

For example, one of the topics on which I present is selling. I've sold. I've read about selling. I've written about selling. I've both attended and presented training sessions and seminars on selling. I've dealt with the subject on numerous occasions in various ways. As a result, I have experience on which to draw to prepare myself for fielding a "pop fly" from an audience on that subject. I prepare by considering two points:

What questions have crossed my mind?

What questions, comments, or objections have I heard from people before?

In a similar manner, you can draw from your experience. After you've outlined a presentation, review your material. Taking one key point at a time, ask yourself those same two questions. You can also draw on the experience of associates or friends. Deliver a dress rehearsal of your presentation to a couple of people. Ask them to jot down questions or concerns that occur to them as you go along. Role-play a question-and-answer session at the end. I'd much rather stumble during a dress rehearsal than on opening night in front of the real audience.

This approach is especially helpful if factors related to the presentation are new to you: the subject, the audience, or your role in the organization. Suppose you're asked to present a quarterly report on departmental performance to the company's board of directors—just two weeks after you've been promoted to head this particular department. If you're not very well acquainted with the operations and you've never appeared before the board before, running your presentation by a couple of associates wouldn't be a bad idea! Drawing on their experience could be very beneficial.

By Anticipating

Experience (whether it's yours or someone else's) helps you anticipate the questions and comments people are likely to raise. In effect, you second-guess them. Not always, but often enough to handle situations better than if you hadn't considered probable audience comments ahead of time.

Write down the questions you think people are likely to ask and the objections that may be raised. Give thought to how you'll respond to each one. Then write your responses down. Practice delivering the responses you've anticipated, just as you would if they were part of your presentation. (They will be if someone asks a question you've anticipated.)

You may even revise the content of your presentation so that it addresses and satisfies some points before they're raised. I've found that to be true with the subjects I present. On the subject of selling, for example, one question that people often asked was, "How do I get past the receptionist to the decision maker?" After I answered the question, a typical comment was, "That doesn't work if you're telemarketing." You don't have to beat me over the head too many times before I get the point. Now, whenever I make a presentation on selling, I cover those two bases before they're brought up by the audience.

You can work points like that into the content pretty easily by presenting them in the form of a rhetorical question. For example: "A question that concerns many salespeople is, '"How on earth do I get past this receptionist to get in and see the real decision maker?"' Then cover that part of the presentation, and follow with, "How does that work for those of you who sell by telemarketing?" Pause, and cover that material.

By phrasing an anticipated question or comment in the form of a rhetorical question, you gain the advantage of using relational techniques. You've also taken the wind out of the sails of someone who was poised to spring with a question or objection.

In this way, you address your listeners as though you've read their minds. Some people will think you're very clever to have anticipated what they were going to say. Others will be impressed or feel encouraged that you relate to them so well.

With a limited time frame or extensive or complex subject matter, you may not be able to cover all the bases. Still, you're better equipped to field questions and comments from the audience when you've anticipated them in advance, and prepared and practiced your responses.

Ball players don't go out for the game without having practiced how to field pop flies beforehand. Neither should you.

Fielding Questions

What's the best way to field people's questions? As with many other aspects of presenting, it depends. Is the question a simple one you can answer succinctly? Or is it a question you don't know the answer to? Is the question valid, expressing a genuine concern? Or is it outlandish, voiced by a troublemaker in the group?

Steps

Whichever it is, when someone asks you a question, follow these four steps.

- 1. Listen.
- 2. Determine.
- 3. Affirm.
- 4. Respond.

Listen   Of all the relational skills you develop as a presenter, one of the most important is listening. Although you do far less listening than speaking, how you listen has two significant effects. One is the effect it has on the audience. Listening attentively sends a signal to people watching you that you're interested in them and what they have to say. If that's what they perceive, they'll hold you in high regard.

The other is the effect it has on how you respond. Some people don't verbalize well and may ask a question that isn't communicated clearly. Others don't hear the meaning that you intend to communicate when you speak. They may ask a well-intentioned question that, on the surface, doesn't seem to make sense. If you're listening carefully, though, you can usually sort through the muddle and provide a satisfactory response.

Listen attentively. Maintain eye contact with the speaker, and observe their expression and demeanor while they speak. Nod your head, slightly, in a manner that suggests, "Yes, I hear you." Visually, convey interest in what the person is saying. In some cases, a smile is appropriate; in others, an expression of genuine concern.

Determine   Questions vary in nature. And questioners vary in intent. Some people ask very tough questions but mean well. Others ask seemingly simple questions with every intention of putting you on the spot.

This is a very good reason for listening attentively. As you listen, mentally determine the nature and intent of the question—before you formulate a response. The determination you make about the question will help you decide on the most appropriate response.

There are times when the appropriate response is to preface your answer with a paraphrase. That is, restate the question in condensed form. Paraphrases are worded along these lines:

"Let me be sure I understand. What you're asking is.... Is that right?"

"Am I correct in understanding that you're concerned about...?"

Paraphrasing is useful when you want to clarify a muddled question and confirm that you understand what the speaker is asking. It's also a technique for conveying to people that you really are listening. And in some instances, it buys you time. You may understand a question clearly. You may know the audience knows you're a good listener. But if you need a precious few more seconds to formulate your response, paraphrasing can gain you that time.

Affirm   As you begin to answer the question, first affirm the person who asked it. If you're in a smaller group in an interactive setting, address people by name. It's a more personal form of recognition. Affirmations signal a positive acknowledgment of the person in statements like these:

"That's an interesting question..."

"You make a good point, Joe..."

"You've obviously given this some thought..."

"I'm glad you brought that to our attention, Jane..."

Affirming people, as you may recall from Chapter 3, is one of a presenter's relational skills. Even when someone's question puts you on the spot or suggests they're not in agreement with you, your objective is to maintain a positive relationship with the audience. That includes everyone. How you respond to one person is perceived by the audience as a whole, and it influences the way they react to you. It's here, perhaps more than in any other aspect of your presentation, that your finesse (or lack of it) shows.

Earlier, I referred to members of an audience as "customers." And the familiar adage, "The customer is always right," applies. In fact, we all know the customer is not always right. The trick is to allow them to perceive that they're right, or at least partially right.

That can be a difficult thing to do, especially with tough questions, offensive objections, or a point of disagreement over a controversial issue. To affirm someone without necessarily agreeing with what they've said, you have to separate how you feel about the person from how you respond to their position on the subject. In other words, while I may not agree with what you're saying, I do agree that you have the right to bring it up. An affirmation before you respond validates the person without implying concurrence with their position.

At the same time, take care not to overdo affirming statements. If your tone of voice or the wording of the affirmation is out of proportion with the point a person's raised, you run the risk of sounding insincere. Worse, you may fuel their fire. Overly enthusiastic affirmations can encourage attention seekers to continue raising questions and objections. And that's the last thing you want to do.

Simple Questions

Having affirmed the person, respond to the question. How you respond depends upon the kind of question it is. If it's a simple question, answer it concisely. A short and to-the-point question deserves a short and straightforward answer.

Every once in a while, you'll hear a pontificator. That's the presenter who takes off on oratorical tangents whenever someone asks a question. Someone might ask something as simple as "Where did you get your overhead projector?" and be exposed to a twenty-minute spiel about the technological development of projection equipment. Somewhere in the pontificator's response lies the answer to the question (maybe). While pontificating may be a good technique for discouraging people from asking questions, it fails to satisfy the audience.

Numerous things can be said on just about any subject. But when a person poses a simple question, remember KISS (Keep It Simple, Speaker).

Not-So-Simple Questions

It's not always possible to keep it simple, because not all questions are simple. The kinds of questions people ask are as diverse as people. They come in all shapes and sizes. Some address larger issues that can't be answered with a single sentence.

After you've listened carefully to the not-so-simple question, offer the most appropriate type of response in the shortest possible time. The not-so-simple question usually requires a multifaceted answer. For example, "What's the best way to field questions?" The simplest answer to that question is, "It depends." But you can hardly stop there. An answer that will satisfy the question will state the options that apply (as this section illustrates). If there are too many facets to relate, confine your answer to the most important two or three.

How extensively you answer the question depends on the setting and on the time that's available. Is the norm in this setting to give a thorough response, or will a summary, "broad brush" answer suffice? In a formal setting where a brief question and answer session is held at the end, your answers should be concise. In more informal, interactive settings, you can elaborate and provide more detailed answers if time allows.

We learn by example. And we can learn some things about fielding questions by watching and listening to how the pros do it. One such example is a presidential press conference. There are few settings where the presenter is put on the spot with questions quite as much as in this one. Notice how answers are given in order to satisfy the questioner. At the same time, unnecessary or irrelevant details aren't added. You can "paint yourself into a corner" or invite still more demanding questions if you elaborate to too great an extent.

Some not-so-simple questions reflect a genuine lack of understanding on the part of the questioner. This confusion may be due to an oversight on your part when you presented the material. If so, respond to the question with a statement of the point you omitted. At other times, a question arises because the person wasn't listening attentively to you. If that's the case, restate your point in a brief review.

A lack of understanding can also result from a difference in the way people think. Some people think in concrete terms. Others think conceptually. In cases like this, your answer should take the form of a clarification. Offer a comparison with something familiar, an analogy to which the person can relate.

Suppose you're delivering a presentation on computer systems. A person you perceive to be an office worker asks, "How does that thing store information?" Your answer could compare storing data in the system with storing documents in an office filing cabinet. Or, a person you perceive to be a homemaker asks, "How does that thing store information?" You could draw an analogy with a cookbook or recipe file. By creating a "word picture" that speaks to people's experience, you can usually clear up the confusion or uncertainty that occasioned the question.

The toughest questions are those that are raised when a person disagrees with your point of view. The difficulty for a presenter lies in the possibility of giving an unpopular answer if you're honest. But I believe presenters should always be honest. If you're not, you could get caught contradicting yourself or talking out of both sides of your mouth. Once you lose your credibility with audiences, you might as well leave the platform and go home.

If you're concerned about your answer to a sticky question, preface your answer with a disclaimer, known in some circles as a "CYA (Cover Your Assets) clause." The technique is essentially the same as "unplugging" and uses statements like these:

"I know there are many different points of view on this issue, and I appreciate that. In my opinion, and I'm going to be candid..."

"Your question raises a good point. This is a matter I've given a lot of thought. And while I suspect not everyone will agree with my opinion, I'm going to give it to you honestly..."

Tough questions arise over more than just controversial issues. The subject you're presenting or your position on it may strike a sore spot in some people. It may relate to a personal matter or workplace situation they're having difficulty dealing with. In such situations, answers need to be given with sensitivity and diplomacy.

I encountered just such a situation presenting sales training to a group that was running disastrously below a hundred percent of quota. The mood in the room was tense, to say the least. The sales manager was unhappy. The salespeople were unhappy. And here was an outsider coming in to tell them how to do their jobs—or so they perceived. Early in the session, I opened the floor to questions. In a very testy tone of voice, one person remarked: "Our appointments are made by telemarketers. It's not our fault when we don't get in to see the decision maker. Don't you think the telemarketers should be doing a better job?"

I knew the answer the person wanted was "Yes." But it was not the answer I could give—honestly. It was also not the answer that would have been in the best interests of the group. I replied: "That's an interesting question. Let me preface my response by saying this. I can give you the answer you want to hear, or I can give you my honest opinion. I understand that you may not agree, but in my experience, the ultimate responsibility for a sale lies with the salesperson. Yes, perhaps the telemarketers could be doing a better job. But no, it's not up to them to see that you get to the decision maker. That's up to you." When we recessed for a coffee break, the person who asked the question came up to me, shook my hand, and said, "Thank you for being straight with me."

This scenario illustrates a couple of additional points about answering questions. For one, relate your answer as opinion: based on experience, what you've observed, what the information indicates. Refrain from responding with words like "I feel." That personalizes your response and in a business setting, it can sound wishy-washy. You want to answer more assertively, in objective terms: based on what you know, on what the evidence shows. (As a senior manager said to me one time: "I'm not interested in how you feel. I want to know what you think.")

The second point is that there are two types of questions: those that are motivated by fact and those that are motivated by feeling. When someone asks a question like, "What's the source of the statistics you cited?" it's a question of fact. Those questions can be fielded with ease. Questions motivated by feelings, on the other hand, need to be heard out and handled with care.

It's tough to give a tough answer to a tough question. But I've found people will be receptive, to you and to your response, if you deal with them with honesty. Present your answers with an attitude that reflects three Cs: caring, candor, and confidence. I haven't seen them miss yet.

Questions You Don't Know the Answer To

Many presenters dread being faced with a question they can't answer. I suspect it has something to do with our cultural preoccupation with perfection. We're assaulted on numerous fronts by pressures to be perfectly right: in the way we look, the things we do, with what we say. If it's wrong not to be right, then we perceive it's somehow also wrong not to know the right answer to every question. In fact, it's more wrong to make up a wrong answer.

When someone poses a question you don't have an answer for, the first thing to do is "'fess up." It's really quite easy to do. After all, what's easier than saying: "That's a good question. I wish I had a good answer. Unfortunately, I don't." Then, try to satisfy the question in some way.

While you may not have the answer on the tip of your tongue, there is an answer somewhere. It may be found among the group. You can elicit responses from other people by asking, "Has anyone in the group had any experience with that?" or "Does anyone here have an answer to that question?"

You may even elicit a response from the person who asked the question, using the boomerang technique. They toss a question to you and it returns to them. It goes like this: (Affirmation) "That's a good question." ('Fess up) "I wish I had a good answer, but I don't." (Boomerang) "Based on your experience, what are your thoughts about that?" Referring questions back—to the group or the questioner—can work to your advantage. It gives you an opportunity to demonstrate your relational skills by recognizing people in the audience.

In some circumstances, the most appropriate response is to offer to find the answer and get back to the person. If you do respond, "I'm sorry, I don't know the answer to your question, but I'll find out and get back to you," be sure that you do.

Fielding Comments

As a presenter, you feed ideas and information to an audience. Comments are the audience's feedback to you. Like questions, they come in different forms and need to be handled with the same kind of care. The first three steps that apply to fielding questions apply to fielding comments as well: (1) listen, (2) determine, and (3) affirm.

Listening attentively when someone offers a comment helps you understand the speaker's intent as well as words. When you correctly identify the nature and intent of the comment, you can offer the most appropriate response. I've seen presenters misinterpret comments that were intended simply to add a point. They treated them as though they were objections, and initiated debate. An incident such as this reflects badly on a presenter and can cause unnecessary discord, all of which could have been avoided by listening attentively.

There are basically three types of comments: those that agree with, those that add to, and those that object to something you've said. Naturally, we'd all prefer the first type. Unfortunately, listeners aren't in a hundred percent agreement with presenters a hundred percent of the time. So we need to be prepared to field objections. But let's consider the comments that are easy to handle first.

Comments of Agreement

When someone offers a comment of agreement, all you have to say in response is "Thank you." A member of the audience remarks, "What you said about such-and-such was so true." And they go on to relate something from their experience. Comments like this are often just a reflection of the person's desire to be heard.

Comments of agreement don't require any response other than "Thank you" or "Thank you for sharing that with the group." Refrain from carrying on a private dialogue with the person who agrees with you, as though you're members of a mutual admiration society. It may be tempting but it's inappropriate since it excludes the rest of the group.

Comments of Addition

When someone makes a comment that adds to a point you've made, again your response should be brief. Acknowledge the validity of the person's comment and thank them for it. For example, suppose the following comment were offered during a presentation on handling audience feedback: "I've found there are times you just have to interrupt a person who talks too long." You'd reply by saying something like: "That's a valid point. Thank you for bringing it up."

Unless the comment reminds you of a significant point you overlooked during your presentation, you don't need to expound on it any further. You don't need to have the last word. Instead, you give recognition to the audience when you respond, "You're absolutely right. Thanks for your input."

Objections

How do you handle objections? In a word: carefully. There are times when a person raises an objection because he or she is a detractor looking to pick a fight (the undesirable behavior discussed in Chapter 7). On the other hand, objections do arise out of genuine differences of opinion.

Genuine objections occur when people speak from facts or experience different from your own, or raise a point you may not have considered. If their tone of voice strikes you as abrasive, it doesn't mean they're looking to pick a fight. They may feel uncomfortable raising an objection or nervous about speaking in front of a group.

Fielding objections requires both discernment and diplomacy. You need to discern the motivation for the objection, and then handle it with tact. Your objective is to dissipate the issue, not to dispute the other person's point of view. Avoid getting caught up in a verbal battle defending your right to be right. Becoming defensive or argumentative will almost always guarantee the loss of your credibility.

There are three appropriate responses to a genuine objection: agree, reapproach, or arbitrate. They share two characteristics: (1) they affirm the person and (2) they alleviate heated emotional reactions—on your part and theirs.

Agree   Much as I might hate to admit it, there are times when someone in the audience makes a point that's more right than mine. If someone objects to something you've said and he or she is right, acknowledge that. You can slip gracefully off the hook by saying something like: "Thank you for bringing that to our attention. I wasn't aware of that latest report." Or simply state, "That's a good point."

Reapproach When someone raises a genuine objection but the point is not valid, try approaching the matter from a different direction. (Sometimes it's not what you say to which people object as much as how you said it.) If they can be brought around to see the point from another perspective, they may come to agree with you.

A reapproach is phrased: "You've brought up an interesting point. However, let's consider this from another angle." Then further explain your point of view in a way other than how you originally presented it. (Don't just keep hammering away at the same point in the same way or emotions will get heated and you'll end up locking horns.) Draw a comparison, make an analogy, or describe a scenario. Express your response in terms they can relate to.

On occasion, an authoritative type of manager will object to the point I make about the importance of relational skills. Their objection goes something like this: "I'm not going to fuss about persuading people. They'll do it because I say so." A reapproach response would be worded along these lines: "I can see what you're saying. However, let's consider this from another angle." (A scenario, related calmly and courteously, follows.) "Imagine that the chief executive of your company calls you into a meeting, and tells you how to run your department." (A rhetorical question draws the objector in.) "How would you feel about that? Now, what if that same executive applied these relational skills: recognized your experience, elicited your input, and related how the procedure applies to you in terms of value. Wouldn't you be more likely to buy in?" In this example, the response to the objection creates an opportunity for the objector to view the point from his or her own perspective.

Should they persist in sticking to their point of view, let the matter drop. It's not worth disrupting your whole presentation for the sake of proving a point. Bring the matter to a close by responding: "Well, as you know, I don't agree; but I can understand your point of view. And I'll be happy to discuss it with you further during the break or after the session."

Arbitrate Objections, especially the more testy ones, can be effectively dispelled using a "feel, felt, found" response. It goes like this: "That's an interesting point. I can understand why you'd *feel* that way. I was talking with someone recently who *felt* the same way, until they *found* that…" What follows "found that…" is a description of something of value in the point you're trying to advance.

For example, suppose you delivered a presentation on personnel management. You impressed upon the audience the importance of creating incentives for employees. Someone in the audience raises the objection: "I'm sick of all this talk about incentives. With the way the costs of business have increased, I can't afford to do any more than I'm already doing." Using the "feel, felt, found" response, you'd say something like: "That's a good point. I can understand why you'd feel that way. In fact, I was talking with a manager recently who felt the same way, until she found that the increase in productivity more than offset the minimal cost of incentives."

The "feel, felt, found" response is a very affirming approach to fielding objections. Introducing the hypothetical third party (the other person who felt the same way) is a means of arbitrating the point of disagreement in a very agreeable way. It lets both you and the person who raised the objection off the hook. You don't have to argue the point to save face.

When people raise a genuine objection, their intent is not to take issue with you, personally. It's likely they're expressing a valid concern, or at least a concern that's valid from their point of view. A disagreement on an issue need not (and should not) occasion disagreement between people.

Effective presenters operate on this principle: It's not as important to prove you're right as it is to stay in the right relationship with the audience. Insistence on being right when a person raises an objection can damage your relationship with people. They "shut down" and stop listening to you. If that happens, you may not get another opportunity to persuade them to your point of view. If, on the the other hand, you place the greater value on keeping the lines of communication open, you may not win this round, but you'll get another chance to get in the ring later on.

These techniques for fielding objections don't guarantee that you'll always be able to gain agreement. However, they do enable you to deal with objections in an agreeable manner. Your listeners will be impressed.

When to Open the Floor

When you open the floor to questions and comments from the audience is up to you. It's one of your points of control as a presenter. While your personal style influences what you're comfortable with, it should be a minor consideration. Accomplished presenters develop an ability to adapt their style to just about any circumstance. The primary consideration, as always, should be, "What will work best in this setting with this subject and this size and type of audience?"

You can open your presentation to audience input at any time: before, during, or after your presentation. As the number of presenters and the occasions for presenting increase, some of the old norms are breaking down. The traditional format for public speaking called for a question and answer session at the end, if at all. But as we understand the importance of interaction with an audience, we recognize that's not always the best format to follow. It has advantages (which we'll consider shortly), but other approaches are preferable in some situations.

Before

You might ask: "When would you ever ask for questions or comments before you present? It just doesn't make sense. You haven't even said anything yet, and you're asking the audience to respond?" Yes.

The following example illustrates one technique for opening the floor to audience feedback before you present.

> SETTING: Informal, interactive
>
> AUDIENCE SIZE: A small group of two to a dozen, depending on how much time you have. You can use this same technique with larger groups by asking for input from a few people selected at random.
>
> SUBJECT: Management (although the approach would work with virtually any subject).
>
> PRESENTER: "Every one of you has had some experience with management. You may be a veteran manager or a new manager. And if you're not a manager yet, you probably have one." (The last line, when delivered with humor, usually evokes a laugh.) "Before I start, I'd like to hear from you on two points. What's one thing you know about management? What's one question or concern you have on the subject?"

If it appears people are reluctant to speak up, you can break the ice by offering the first response.

> PRESENTER: "Having been a manager, one thing I know is that it's a tough job. One concern I have is that people receive the training that equips them to do the job well."

When you start the group off in this manner, it gives people time to think of how they're going to respond so they're more at ease doing so. It also gives you an opportunity to make a point.

If you're using name cards or know the names of people in the group, you can then put the ball in their court by saying, "Chris, what are your thoughts on this?" If you don't know names, just start with the first person on your left and go around the group in clockwise order. As people respond, jot down key words on a flip chart or visual board for later reference.

Soliciting people's questions and comments before you present has a number of advantages. For one, it's very relational. From the outset, you're recognizing people's presence and giving them an opportunity to participate. Rather than presenting yourself as the expert, you're acknowledging their experience. I have yet to present to a group that didn't like that. It wins most people over right away.

It also draws out some questions and concerns in advance of your presenting. Forewarned is forearmed. With input from the group, you can make a transition statement into your presentation that incorporates some of their comments. As you do, be sensitive to the points they've raised and be flexible in adapting to the terminology they used.

Suppose the first key point of your presentation was about employee relations. A few people in the group made comments concerning some of the items you're going to cover, but they referred to them as "personnel problems." Revise your wording accordingly. For example, "You've raised some of the very points we'll be covering today. We'll start by exploring an area that's a common concern for managers: how to handle some of these personnel problems." When you say "these," refer to the notes you wrote on the flip chart or visual board as people were giving you their responses, pointing to those that are applicable.

The greatest advantage of inviting input from people before you present is that it prepares you to field questions or concerns you may not have anticipated in advance. Now that you've heard some comments from the audience, you can start thinking about how you're going to handle them.

Will inviting input from the audience before you present bring out every question or objection? Probably not. But it does help to open up the audience. And it can serve to break down the resistance some people may have brought to the meeting with them. When you indicate early on that you're willing to listen, people often respond in kind. They'll be more receptive to you and less offensive with objections later on.

This first example described how a presenter might invite audience input in a direct manner. In other words, the audience is asked directly to respond directly. In more formal, proactive settings, this same technique can be used by posing rhetorical questions.

A presentation might be opened in this way: "Every one of you has had some experience with management. You may be a veteran manager or a new manager. And if you're not a manager yet, you probably have one. What are some of the questions and concerns you've had about management?" (A rhetorical question. Pause briefly, then continue.)

"When I talk with managers like yourselves, some of the most common concerns they voice are these. How can I demonstrate effective leadership? What can I do to increase productivity? How do I motivate people?"

Naturally, the rhetorical questions you pose would be related to the key points you're going to cover. If you understand your subject and the way it relates to your audience, you'll see people in the audience nodding their heads in agreement as you speak. Even when the approach is only rhetorical, the relational effect is much the same. The audience perceives that you understand and "hear" their concerns, albeit vicariously.

Whether you do it directly or rhetorically, eliciting audience responses at the beginning of a presentation can be an effective technique. What about during a presentation?

During

Asking for comments or questions during a presentation applies only to interactive settings. The time frame needs to be sufficient to allow for input from the audience; and the format of the occasion must be such that participation is an accepted norm. Giving a fifteen minute speech at a service club luncheon doesn't qualify. Delivering a one-hour sales presentation might. Presenting a half-day seminar does. Even then, there are drawbacks and limitations.

During the body of a presentation, comments from the audience can be interruptive. They can disrupt the orderly flow of your message, and they take up time. Nevertheless, including the audience has great relational value, especially during lengthier presentations.

The best time to invite comments or questions is after you've completed each key point, so you and your listeners don't lose the "train of thought." After taking comments and questions from the floor, make a transition statement before you resume. This brief summary and preview will help to bring the audience back on track with your subject.

A potential drawback to taking comments during the course of a presentation is the risk of losing control of people in the group and of the time. Phrases like these can help you manage both:

"In the ten minutes remaining before we take a break, what questions do you have?"

"Based on the information we've considered, what are your thoughts on Point A?" When the time you allotted for comments is up, state, "You've raised some very good points and I'm sure there are more. But in view of the time we need to move on."

"We can take just one more question before we go on with Point B."

When you invite feedback in an interactive setting during your presentation, a debate may arise between two or three people. As the presenter (group leader), you want to assert yourself and bring it to an end, especially if time is running out. Intervene by saying something like: "I appreciate your obvious enthusiasm for this subject. You both have some valid points. If we move on and consider the rest of the material, I think we'll resolve some of the issues you've raised."

Some presentations and settings aren't suited to questions or comments from the audience during the presentation. Typically, that would be true of more formal speeches, larger audiences, shorter time frames, or all of the above. In those cases, questions and comments are deferred until the end of the presentation, or they're not solicited at all

After

Let the audience know at the outset if you're going to handle questions at the end. After the introductory portion of your presentation (after you've stated your opener, objective, and preview), simply add a statement, "I'll be happy to answer any questions you may have at the end of the program."

When you defer audience feedback, be sure you end your presentation early enough to allow sufficient time for people's questions and comments. If you've announced you're going to give people a chance to speak, you need to give them the time to do so.

When you open the floor to audience feedback, do so in the form of an open question, e.g., "What questions or comments do you have?" Then retain your composure while you pause long enough to give members of the audience a chance to speak up. In ninety-nine presentations out of a hundred, you'll hear the presenter ask, "Do you have any questions?" The question is often posed in a tone of voice that implies the answer is "No" (because the presenter doesn't want to have to answer any). The open form of question implies you're more receptive to the audience.

Most people I know would prefer occupying the floor exclusively when they present. It's much easier to get up, deliver your message, and sit down again—without eliciting audience feedback. As soon as people are invited to respond, a presenter has to deal with the unexpected.

You may be able to predict some questions and objections based on experience and by anticipating. But you never know when someone will raise a point you weren't prepared for. By listening attentively, responding affirmatively, and managing your emotions and the relationship with the group, even tough questions and objections can be fielded skillfully.

To Field Like a Pro, Remember

- Anticipate probable questions and comments in advance, and prepare responses to them.

- There are three steps in responding:

Listen	Attentively.
Affirm	"That's a good question." "You've raised an interesting point."
Determine	The nature and intent of the question. The most appropriate response. Paraphrase to clarify or buy time.

- Field questions as follows:

Simple	Keep your answer simple, concise.
Not-so-simple	Relate the important two or three facets; or Give a brief summary review of the point; or Clarify with a comparison or scenario.
Don't know	'Fess up. Refer the question to the group. "Boomerang" back to the questioner. Offer to find the answer and get back.
In every case	Answer with caring, candor, and confidence.

- Field comments as follows:

Of agreement	"Thank you."
Of addition	Acknowledge the point; thank the speaker.
Objection	Agree, reapproach, or arbitrate.

9
Skill-Building Resources

The demand for skilled presenters has grown in recent years, and it continues to increase. As business becomes more and more competitive, people adept at presenting to customers are an invaluable resource. More community education, professional development, and group support programs are founded every day. Every one of them requires a staff of accomplished facilitators and presenters. Our educational systems and corporate training departments are being evaluated with an eye to results achieved. Skilled presenters are an integral part of the process of producing improved results. In almost every arena—business, politics, education, religion, social action—the person who can present, powerfully and persuasively, is a distinct asset.

Where do you go to develop, practice, and perfect your skills? With all the resources available today, your options are numerous.

Speakers' Groups

If you're new to presenting or feel awkward about it, joining a speakers' group can be a good place to start building both your skills and confidence. You'll find them in almost every community. One of the most well known is Toastmasters. They meet specifically for the purpose of developing speaking skills, and they are accustomed to welcoming novice presenters. Not only can you gain exposure to public speaking techniques, but you'll gain encouragement from the practice and peer support as well.

A local chapter of the American Society for Training and Development (ASTD) may also be an appropriate avenue if your occupation or interests involve human resource development. Meeting agendas often include presentations on subjects such as communications and group facilitation skills that are of interest to speakers. The ASTD also provides opportunities to meet professionals who are in positions that involve presenting and to observe presentations by "role model" speakers.

Training and Coaching

There are numerous courses available for training in presenting and public speaking. Some are provided by corporate human resource departments. Others are offered at junior colleges, universities, and through community adult education classes. Some are available on audio or videocassette programs.

Whichever form of training you choose, look for training that emphasizes presenting (as opposed to public speaking). If the training is given in person, look for an instructor who's a skilled presenter, not an academician. Select training that emphasizes practical applications, not a textbook approach. And be sure the training gives you opportunities to get up on your feet and present yourself. You'll learn far more by actually doing it than you will by listening to lectures.

Real skill development is a process that occurs over time. While you're going through the process (whether it's two days or two weeks), work with an instructor or an associate who can serve as a coach. Your skills will improve remarkably with personalized guidance, appropriate feedback, and encouragement.

One of the gratifications of learning, and teaching, how to present is that you see improvement in a short period of time. With proper instruction, coaching, review, and feedback, even weak presenters can become optimum presenters in a matter of a few days or weeks.

Taping

Although it was more years ago than I like to remember, I can still recall my first training in presentation skills. Everyone in the class delivered a presentation which the group then critiqued. Someone mentioned that I rocked on my feet. Of course, I didn't believe it. I mean, if you rocked on your feet, surely you'd know it.

Later, the group met to view videotapes that had been made of our presentations. You can imagine my surprise when, yes, there I stood, rocking on my feet. Seeing that videotape made such an impression on me that it wasn't long before I stopped rocking.

Videotaping is used by professionals in many fields to observe performance and spot areas for improvement. It's an excellent form of skill evaluation and development that should augment basic skills training. By videotaping your presentations, you'll be able to hear and see yourself the way others hear and see you. If you don't have video equipment available, the next best thing is to record your presentations on audiocassette. You'll still be able to tell a lot about how you're presenting just from the way you sound.

Find a partner to work with (a professional coach or associate). A partner helps to objectify the way you view yourself, so you don't fall prey to being your own worst critic. While you deliver a presentation, have your partner tape you. Afterward, review the videotape (or audiocassette) together. When you do so, look for the skills and techniques covered in this book. (Use the Presentation Review Checklist in the appendix as a guide to self-evaluation.)

When you evaluate your presentations, take care to observe the good points as well as those that could be improved. Remember, "Accentuate the positive, eliminate the negative." Don't focus exclusively on what you observe to be negative. Accentuate your positive points as well. They provide the fuel that feeds your enthusiasm to further develop your skills.

Developing and evaluating your presentation skills can be approached in one of two ways. One approach entails taping the same presentation in three subsequent stages. During the first stage, concentrate on the organization of your material. In the second, add relational techniques. For the third, add delivery skills and audiovisual media to complete your presentation in its entirety. This is a "building block" approach best suited to people new to presenting.

The second is more suited to people who have presented but want to improve their skills. Deliver and tape your whole presentation. After reviewing the first taping, select one or two points you want to improve. Concentrate on refining just those techniques. Then, present and tape again. Congratulate yourself on the improvements you've made. If needed, repeat the process. Eventually, you'll develop a presentation that will satisfy even the toughest critic.

Sales Training

Even if you're not in a sales position and never intend to be, selling skills can be applied to many different situations. Presenting is one of them.

The best presenters are persuasive. The best presenters understand how to deal with people and how to relate value to them. There's no better place to learn those skills than in a good sales training program.

Good sales training also teaches effective questioning techniques and how to overcome objections. If you present in smaller-group, interactive settings, developing those skills is absolutely essential.

Stage Experience

I attribute much of my comfort level with presenting to having studied dance as a youngster. Early on, I was acclimated to being on stage and appearing before groups of strangers. I suspect the experience accounts for my view that presenting is enjoyable and audiences are non-threatening.

One thing you'll observe in skilled presenters is that they appear, from time to time, to ham it up. They're articulate, expressive, emotive, and artful at playing to audiences. They approach presenting as an entertainer approaches acting. When the subject is light, they have a good time presenting. So the audience has a good time, too. When the subject is serious, they're involved in the material. So the audience gets involved, too.

I'm sure I've shocked some clients when I've suggested they enroll in an acting class or take part in an amateur theater group. More than once that suggestion has been met with expressions of disbelief by mature and serious-minded professional people. They'll go to a graduate business school to obtain an M.B.A. and take classes in statistics and theory they may never apply. But they wouldn't dream of taking an acting class that would help develop skills they could use with people every day.

Any stage experience that helps you relate to an audience, comfortably, will help improve the way you present. Through repeated exposure, you'll gain expressiveness. You'll develop a confident stage presence and overcome any stage fright. You'll become less conscious of yourself as you learn to step into the role of another. And presenting is very much like role playing.

A further advantage to getting involved in an activity like this is that, for the amateur, it's recreational. You enroll in a business class and what happens? You feel the pressure of having to make the grade. But enroll in an acting class and what happens? You have fun! Instead of adding to the stress you may already have, it can actually serve to relieve it.

Role Models

The material on platform behavior in Chapter 4 touched on the value of observing skilled presenters and emulating their platform behavior. You can see and hear excellent presenters through any number of different sources: on audiocassette and videotape programs, television broadcasts, at conferences and conventions, in seminars and workshops, and sometimes at meetings right in your own office.

In almost every endeavor we undertake, we can take cues from those who exhibit enviable skill. I recall the most wonderful day skiing, when I skied better than I ever did before (or since). I was following an expert skier down the slopes. It was a lesson in the value of role models. When I reflect on how I present today, I see in my presentations techniques that I've borrowed from expert presenters.

A novice presenter listening to a "role model" presenter is sometimes tempted to say, "I could never present like that!" If you've read Chapter 7 on overcoming anxiety, you know you're giving yourself a negative message. Change it into a self-affirmation, "I can present like that!"

Yes, you can. Find yourself a good role model or two. As you emulate what they do, you'll find your own skills start mirroring theirs. Then, you'll be a role model for someone else.

Opportunities

One of the best resources for building presentation skills is, simply, to present. Present, and present, and present. With each subsequent presentation you can add to your repertoire of techniques and reinforce your skills.

Although every workplace is different, most have occasions when groups meet and someone presents. Be alert to those that occur in your organization. If someone is needed to chair a meeting, volunteer. If someone is needed to announce a new procedure or product line, offer to make the presentation. Whatever the occasion—welcoming a new employee, delivering a report to the management committee, kicking off a community fund-raising campaign—every opportunity to present represents an opportunity to build your skills.

If you're currently in an occupation or a workplace that doesn't provide chances for you to present, then seek your opportunities else-

where. Business, trade, and professional organizations often welcome
guest speakers (provided you have something to say), in order to fill
program agendas. Social action agencies and churches often need volunteers who can deliver community awareness programs or present to
classes.

Repeatedly getting up on your feet and presenting is the surest way
of furthering your abilities. Then one day you realize you're no longer
practicing. You've mastered the skills of presenting. When that happens, you'll no longer need resources—other than additional opportunities to present for the fun of it!

To Build the Skills of a Pro, Remember

- Take advantage of the many resources that are readily available:

  Speakers' groups
  Training and coaching
  Taping (videotaping or audiocassette)
  Sales training
  Stage and audience experience
  Role models
  Opportunities to present

10
Q's and A's

It's customary to have a question and answer period at the end of a presentation. This is it. It's my hope this book has answered most of the questions you might have had about presenting. However, that's also my hope whenever I teach on the subject. Invariably, there are additional points that surface at the end.

Many of the answers reflect two factors inherent in my "philosophy" about presenting. One is that, regardless of which side of the podium or platform they're on, people are people. And we get on best when we relate to one another. (Thus a presenter gets on best with an audience when he or she relates to them). When a student or client asks me a question about presenting, my response is often a question in return: "What would you do if you were talking just to me, one on one?"

The other factor is common sense. When a situation arises and you're not sure what to do, ask yourself, "What makes the most sense?" Should I use a visual here? "What makes the most sense?" Which point should I make first? "What makes the most sense?" How do I answer their question? "What makes the most sense?"

It's a sounding board that works for almost every situation. And it works especially well in combination with the first factor. In other words, what makes the most sense—in relation to these people.

Other questions may come up after you set this book down and go off to pursue opportunities to present. If you keep these two factors in mind, you'll be able to answer most of them for yourself.

What follows are some questions compiled from real, live students and clients. I appreciate their contributions.

Question: I make formal speeches from behind a podium. It isn't appropriate to move around and I can't use visual aids. How can I make my speeches more expressive and interesting?

Answer: One of the most captivating speakers I've had the pleasure to watch and listen to was a woman who had been crippled and blinded in an accident. She was helped to the podium and had to hold onto it for support. The only physical means she had at her disposal for giving expression to her message were her face and her voice. She used both wonderfully! She did have one advantage over a sighted speaker: she couldn't read from notes.

For starters, know your subject well enough that you can speak with self-assurance. Project to the audience without having to look down and rely constantly on notes. Your eyes can express a great deal, provided the audience can see them. Eyes sparkle and widen with excitement. Brows furrow with serious concern. You can inject meaning and interest through your facial expressions, hand gestures, and the tone and inflections in your voice (see Chapter 4).

Yes, you can move. While you may not be free to step out from behind the podium, you can use the movement of your head and hands and body. Step back, step forward, lean to one side or another. To illustrate: Picture yourself at the podium. One moment, you're standing back about six inches from the edge of the podium with an upright posture, hands resting on either side with arms outstretched. What expression does that give your message? A moment later, you've moved close up, elbows resting on the podium, leaning slightly forward, occasionally gesturing with one hand. See how that changes the impression you're conveying?

And, yes, you can use visual aids. Your natural attributes (as described above) are audiovisuals. You can use them to your advantage. You can describe some content very visually with scenarios and word pictures. And you can use media visuals as well. You may just have to be a bit more creative than the presenter who can use a whole stage.

For example, during a televised presentation, former President Reagan delivered a formal speech from behind a podium and used a very effective visual aid. He was speaking on the subject of the federal budget. To emphasize a point about the budget and the extent of expenditures, he held up one section after another. Reams and stacks and volumes of pages. It was a very effective visual aid for emphasizing his point.

On another occasion I observed a presentation about interpersonal communications. The presenter used this visual aid: two tin cans connected by a piece of string. Easy to use from behind a podium.

Even so-called formal speeches can be more expressive and interesting. You can give vocal and visual expression to your feelings and thoughts, and be creative about to what objects illustrate your main points.

Question: What should I do with my hands? I feel like my arms are just hanging at my sides and I don't know what to do with them.

Answer: Aside from gesturing with them when it's appropriate, using your hands depends on where you're delivering your presentation from. If you're speaking from behind a podium, avoid clutching the sides of the podium in a kind of death grip. That's a sure sign of nervousness. Relax at the elbows, and rest your hands—on the sides of the podium or the top surface nearest you. If you're using note cards or pages, you might hold the outer edges of those—much as newscasters do—in a relaxed and comfortable manner.

If you're speaking from the front of a room, entirely visible to the audience, try bending your arms at the elbows and resting them loosely against your waist (as though your hands were resting in your lap if you were seated). Bring your hands together and either cross your fingers, touch fingertips together, or rest one hand inside the other. Held in this manner, you can easily open your hands up to gesture, then bring them back together again.

Question: Is it true you shouldn't put your hands in your pockets?

Answer: As with many other aspects of presenting, that depends on what you want the audience to perceive.

When people put their hands in their pockets, it usually signifies one of three things. They're nervous and they rattle keys and coins (very distracting!). They feel awkward and don't know what to do with their hands. Or, they're relaxed and they want to send a signal to the audience to relax, too.

If you're putting your hands in your pockets for the first two reasons, then, yes, it's true. Keep your hands out of your pockets. But, if you're intentionally putting your hands in your pockets as a means of conveying a message, then, no, it's not true. It's not only permissible to put your hands in your pockets, but it serves a purpose as well.

When you want an audience to perceive you as an authority, your hands should be out of your pockets. When you want to add meaning to your message through gestures, your hands have to be out of your pockets. (It's awfully hard to gesture if they're not.) On the other hand (no pun intended), when you want to relax the tone of your presentation or be perceived as "just one of the folks," putting your hands in your pockets (briefly) can create that effect. With gestures and movements, you can either call the audience to "stand at attention," or use a gesture that signals "at ease." Putting your hands in your pockets puts them at ease (provided it's done in moderation).

Question: Do you ever draw a blank? How do you handle it if you do?

Answer: Yes, my mind does go blank, sometimes right in the middle of a sentence. When it happens, I handle it as I try to handle other misadventures: with humor, when it's appropriate.

One of the things that bothers some people when they present is a fear that the audience is something other than human. They're not. An audience is nothing more than a composite of human beings just like you. If your mind goes blank and my mind goes blank, then the chances are very good that their minds go blank on occasion, too.

My response is difficult to describe in words alone, so I'm going to ask you to visualize. What would you do if you were talking just to me and your mind suddenly went blank? Your physical reaction would probably be something like this. Your head would bow in a manner that suggests you're thinking, and you might raise a hand to your forehead. Then you'd raise your head and look at me with a somewhat puzzled expression. You'd say, with a kind of quizzical smile, "I just drew a blank." (All of that would happen within a nanosecond.)

That's exactly what I've done in front of an audience: "I just drew a blank." I might add, with a slight nod of my head, "Does that ever happen to you?" (People in the group nod in agreement. They empathize.) By then, I've recovered the thought, "Ah, yes, as I was saying before my brain went on the blink..." (They laugh.) And I go on.

Question: How do I get people to sit toward the front of the room?

Answer: Be at the location for your presentation fifteen minutes to a half-hour before you're scheduled to start. As people come in, introduce yourself and initiate conversation in a friendly tone of voice so they begin to feel more comfortable with you. You can either encourage them to take a seat up front (verbally); or literally usher them to the front row. Explain they'll be better able to hear and see your presentation from there. If they're reluctant, say, "I'd appreciate it if you did. I'd like to leave some seats in the back free for late arrivals so they don't interrupt the session once we get started."

Question: What's the best way to introduce a subject?

Answer: There are any number of ways to introduce the topic of a presentation. (See Chapter 2, "Preparing Your Message," for a description of openers.)

In general, the best way to start is with something that will immediately capture people's attention. Specifically, you might open with a relevant anecdote, scenario, a quotation from a recognized authority, a startling or dramatic statistic or declarative statement, or a rhetorical question. Try combining two or three of these forms.

When you're outlining your presentation, write out two or three alternative openers. Read them back to yourself or to someone else, aloud. Which one gets your attention? Which one will most appeal to people and speak to them "where they live" (i.e., at the "gut" level, in their hearts)?

The worst way to introduce a subject is the old fashioned way: "Good morning, my name is…I want to talk to you about…" There's nothing very enticing in that form of introduction.

Question: I hear speakers who say things like "er," "um," "okay," and "you know" a lot. They don't seem to be aware of it, but it's distracting when you're listening. How can I tell if I'm doing that? If I am, how can I correct it?

Answer: You can find out everything you always wanted to know but were afraid to ask through the magic of modern technology. Next time you present, make arrangements to have your presentation videotaped or recorded on audiocassette. If you don't have access to video or audio equipment, then ask a friend or coworker for a helpful critique.

If you are inserting fillers when you speak, just hearing yourself present will be a major step toward improving. Remind yourself you don't need to talk nonstop. That's usually the reason people insert "ers" and "ums."

Practice bringing every sentence to a complete stop when you speak. Breathe. Pause. Begin the next sentence. When you use this technique, it will seem stilted at first. But gradually one sentence will flow into another, without those distracting fillers in between. (See Chapter 4 on optimizing your effectiveness.)

Question: I make speeches on a very sensitive subject and I don't want to offend or alienate people. What's the best way to open my presentations to win the audience over right away?

Answer: You'll win people over more by how you say something than by what you say. If you deal with a sensitive subject with obvious sensitivity, the audience is likely to respond favorably.

Look for some aspect of your subject that appeals to people in a nonthreatening way and develop a means for expressing that aspect. For example, what human interest story could you open with and then relate to your topic? What personal experience could you describe in a gracious and personable way? What creative and pleasing visual would capture the point and their attention?

After you've stated your opener, you might express your concern for people's feelings in a straightforward manner. I don't see anything wrong in saying something like: "I know this is a sensitive subject. Some of you might even prefer not hearing about it, and I can understand that. However, (state the subject) affects (so many/all) of our lives that I would encourage you to set aside your initial reactions and explore this issue objectively with me."

Question: How do I decide how many main points I should have, and how fully I should develop each one?

Answer: Remember the rule of three (see Chapter 2 on preparing your message). The time and circumstances of your presentation influence how many points you relate and in how much detail. If you have only ten minutes to speak, you may decide to address only one significant point and highlight just two or three supporting items. If you're delivering a half-day seminar, you may have the opportunity to deliver three main points and explore each one extensively. If the time frame is the same in both proactive and interactive settings, you'll have less time to develop each point in detail in the interactive setting since you need to allow for audience participation.

Question: How do I know if I have too many audiovisuals? How do I know if I don't have enough?

Answer: There's no simple formula like "Ten percent of your presentation should be visuals." It varies with the many factors you have to take into account: time frame, setting, the nature of your subject, the type of visuals you're using, and what you're comfortable with.

The main rule of thumb to bear in mind is that the purpose of audiovisuals is to support and enhance the presentation of the subject, not to replace it. (See Chapter 5, "Media Make a Difference.")

If you get the feeling you're spending too much time and attention on audiovisuals and not enough on your audience, you probably are. Take a few audiovisuals out and see if it works better. If you feel there's a point the audience would better understand and remember if it were visualized, then add a visual aid there.

Question: I work with a couple of people who regularly present at meetings. I don't think they realize they're not very good. What should I say to them?

Answer: I feel like "Dear Abby" on this one. I'd avoid saying anything to them. I wouldn't praise a presentation when it's not praiseworthy.

You might suggest to the appropriate manager that a seminar in presentation skills would be beneficial for the office staff and good for the business. Or (she said with humor), hand out copies of this book as birthday or Christmas gifts.

Question: I'm self-conscious about presenting because I speak with an accent. Is there anything I can do?

Answer: This is a question that warrants a two-part answer.

First, I wouldn't be self-conscious about speaking with an accent. There are hundreds of very successful people in this country who present and speak with an accent: Henry Kissinger, Dr. Ngor, and Eva Gabor, to name a few. Some people even work at retaining their accents and turn their speech to their advantage. An accent can be perceived as a characteristic that distinguishes you from the norm.

If you do want to diminish your accent, remember, we're influenced by the input we receive. One type of input is sound. So try this technique. Obtain a videotape or cassette recording of someone whose voice and articulation are pleasing to you. Listen to it. Listen again. And listen some more. As you listen, stop periodically and repeat the speaker's words aloud. Concentrate on speaking more slowly and deliberately. Gradually, you'll find your own speech patterns taking on some of the characteristics of your "media mentor."

Question: I'm so nervous when I have to make a presentation that my hands visibly shake. What can I do?

Answer: First, practice techniques for overcoming anxiety. (See Chapter 8.) Be sure to be well prepared before presenting. The more confident you are about what you're going to say, the more relaxed you'll be.

If you know anyone in the audience, begin by looking to them for encouraging nonverbal feedback: a smile, a nod of agreement, an expression of interest. If you don't know anyone in the audience, look for a kindly face or two that makes you feel more at ease. (Just be careful you don't address them exclusively.)

To keep your hands from shaking, you might try holding a pen: one hand holding one end, the other hand holding the other. (Not grasping or clutching, just holding it easily.) Be careful that you don't twist and turn and fiddle with it, or it will be distracting to the audience.

Try adopting a conversational mode. Some of your nervousness may be caused by a common misperception that a presentation has to be formal. It doesn't. In fact, the best presentations usually aren't.

Question: I'm basically a shy and quiet person. I feel enthusiastic but I don't show it. I know my material is very well organized. What can I do to present with more enthusiasm?

Answer: One thing I've observed in people who are shy is a tendency to avoid eye contact with the audience. If they're speaking from a podium, they generally look down at their notes—even if they don't need to refer to them. If they're speaking from the front of a room, they look over the heads in the audience or concentrate on their visuals. An audience won't perceive much enthusiasm from a presenter who's not "connecting" with them. Work on projecting out to the audience and maintaining focused eye contact.

After you've outlined your presentation, talk about it to someone you're comfortable with to work up expressions of enthusiasm. Just before you present, think about what most enthuses you, what you really want to get across. How does that make you feel? Imagine conveying that same feeling to other people. Concentrate on that good feeling, not the fear.

Question: I'd like to have every one of the people on my staff trained to give better presentations. I can't afford to pay educational reimbursement for all of them to attend classes. If I brought a trainer in to do an on-site seminar, I can't have all of them away from their jobs at the same time. What would you suggest?

Answer: Try a "train the trainer" approach. Let your staff know what you're interested in doing (for their benefit). Tell them you're looking for someone who will serve as an in-house trainer. The person who volunteers is likely to share your interest in presenting. Just make sure he or she also has the attributes for the job.

Provide training and coaching for that individual. Once they're trained, you can then develop an in-house training program within your budget and scheduling requirements. Select media that can supplement your program and facilitate the trainer's job: books, audiocassettes, videotapes.

Question: Have you ever had an embarrassing moment when you were presenting? How did you handle it?

Answer: Now this is an easy question. Yes, I've had embarrassing moments. I think every presenter does. In fact, you could probably create a counterpart to "TV's Bloops and Blunders" from presenters' embarrassing moments.

How do you handle it? Quickly, with humor. Laughter is a great tension-reliever—for presenters and for audiences alike. You can get past most embarrassments with a brief and amusing remark. Then move right along to the next thing on your agenda.

Don't draw attention to it. Don't apologize for it (unless it's affected someone who deserves an apology). And by all means, don't accentuate it by making the moment out to be bigger than it is. I've had instances when I've said or done something that was embarrassing; and half the audience wasn't even aware of it.

Don't be afraid of being embarrassed. It goes with the territory, so to speak. And don't let fear of embarrassment stand in the way of presenting. If you take your chances and get up on your feet with a well-prepared and practiced presentation, you have far more to gain than to lose.

Question: I make presentations to small groups in management and customer meetings. What can I do to make my presentations distinct from all the others they see and hear?

Answer: If you apply all the practices described in this book, your presentations will be distinctive. Pay particular attention to the things that are very obvious to your audience. For example, visual aids should reflect the creativity and quality you want to communicate. Be sure they're graphic and colorful (but not garish). If you distribute handouts, have them professionally prepared. And personalize them with company or participant names.

What distinguishes your house from your neighbor's? The little personal touches. Whenever I present to small groups seated at tables, I arrange "place settings" in advance. I set tent cards with people's names already written on them and a small personal-sized note pad and a brand-new sharpened pencil at each place. A folder for handouts is placed under the note pad. And between every two settings, I place a small clear plastic container with assorted Life Savers and mints. (It's amazing how many people remark on those and ask if they can take the leftovers home.) I make sure that fresh hot coffee and tea, as well as cold water, are available on a credenza nearby.

One last note. Let people know they're important enough to you for you to be prepared for them. Arrive well enough in advance to have everything set up and arranged and to ensure that you're calm, cool, and collected when you start. There's nothing more disruptive than a presenter who dashes in at the last moment. It gives the impression that this presentation is disrupting your schedule. Instead, you want to create the impression that you're happy to be there, paying special attention to your listeners.

Question: How does a person ever put together everything it takes to become a really accomplished presenter?

Answer: One skill at a time, bit by bit. In many ways, presenting is like skiing. The pros make it look so easy. But the first time you try to get up and do it yourself, you realize there's a lot more to it than meets the eye.

I remember when I first took to the slopes. I stood at the base of the mountain watching the experts ski down. It was breath-taking, inspiring. I was enthralled. I thought how much I'd like to be able to ski like that.

At the time, I was dating an expert skier so I had the motivation. I could appreciate the importance of learning the basics, so I took classes and received coaching. I had my share of nasty spills, of course (everyone does at first). But I was encouraged every time I made it down a hill and observed other novices trying it, too.

The first time I took the lift to the top of an expert run, I was terrified. The fear of speaking before groups is nothing compared to the fear I felt pushing off down that mountain! But I was in the company of good friends and better skiers. I determined to overcome the fear and follow the pros. I did it. Not expertly. But well enough to experience the excitement and satisfaction that spurred me to do it again.

When you first begin to ski, you wonder, "How will I ever put all of this together?" And then one day, you do it—without thinking. Presenting is just like that. And you approach it the same way. To do it expertly requires motivation, training, and practice. To do it enjoyably, you have to overcome your fears and present until you experience success. You concentrate on trying one new skill, on adding one new technique at a time. Then one day, you deliver that near-perfect presentation—without even thinking about it. At that moment you experience the excitement and satisfaction that comes from presenting like a pro!

Epilogue

You've just delivered a presentation. The meeting breaks for coffee. Outside in the hallway, you overhear someone say, "That speaker had such charisma!" How do you feel being described as a person with charisma?

Charisma is a rare quality. We reserve the word for people we perceive to be spirited and enthusiastic. People with charisma have a unique ability to move us, an ingenious power to persuade. They're the ones who get ahead.

Charisma is derived from a Greek word that means "gift" or "favored." Do you have the gift of oratory? Have you been favored with the physical attributes of a naturally commanding presence? If so, then you're a natural-born speaker—and you're one in a million. (You probably didn't need this book at all.)

But if, like most of us, your answer is "No," then this next principle is for you:

> Inside every person there's a potential presenter. Inside every presenter there's the potential to present like a pro!

There are pros in every field of endeavor: in sports, in the arts, in business. They weren't born that way. They got that way through training, experience, and practice. They make what they do look easy. Not because it is; and not because they're specially gifted to do it. They make it look easy because they want to do it, and they've tried it until they got it right.

I've seen and heard some wonderfully gifted presenters during the course of my career—presenters who were real pros. Some had a gift for humor; others naturally cared about people. Some were favored with a quick mind, others with a heart full of concern over an issue. Some were gifted with a technical aptitude or an ability related to their business. All had to develop the skills of making effective presentations.

I have one last story, about L., a student in one of my courses. She had come to the United States from the Orient to complete her college education. Having spoken English for only about a year and half, she had a noticeable accent and some difficulty choosing the right words. She was a tiny thing in her early twenties. Standing under five feet tall, she barely peered over the top of a podium. No matter. She was so shy she stayed behind it for security and couldn't bring herself to look at the group. I will leave it to you to imagine what L.'s first presentation was like. Hardly what you would describe as effective.

I must have done a pretty fair job persuading the class early on of the value of presentation skills. L. wanted to succeed in the course and with her business aspirations, and she made a tremendous effort. When she delivered her final presentation, just four weeks later, it was like observing the difference between night and day. On a scale of one to a hundred, her "charisma rating" had improved a hundred percent! She stepped out from behind the podium and made meaningful eye contact with the group. She was expressive, and sincere, and obviously committed to the import of her message. L. was gifted with a will to succeed. I was persuaded by her last presentation. I was persuaded that anyone can present with charisma if they want to enough.

Presenters with charisma are people who augment whatever attributes they have by learning how to present them. Like L., we all have attributes of one sort or another. Our "charisma rating" is a reflection of how much we want to communicate to others—what we are, what we know, what we care about.

One of the challenges of delivering a message about presenting is that people expect you to follow your own advice. So, in keeping with my model outline, here's your closing "to do." Make this commitment:

> I will prepare a presentation and deliver it, using the relational skills, delivery techniques, and audiovisual aids that are the hallmarks of an effective presentation.

Then follow these guidelines:

P   Practice, practice, practice.

R   Respect the time you've been given to speak.

E   Expect an enjoyable experience.

S   Stimulate the audience and seek their response.

E   Enthuse, energize, and encourage.

N   Never open with a joke.

T   Try…train…tape…and test your skills.

What's in it for you? One day you'll overhear someone saying: "There's a presenter with charisma! There's a real pro!"

Appendix

The worksheets that follow are designed to make it easier to develop an effective presentation, keeping in focus significant principles and techniques.

Contents

Preplanning Worksheet

Model Outline Worksheet

Presentation Review Checklist

Preplanning Worksheet

For Topic _____ Date _____

Contact _____ Phone _____

Objective _____ No. Expected _____

Time Frame _____ Start At _____ Finish By _____

Mode/Setting __ Proactive/ Formal __ Interactive/Informal _____

Audiovisual Equipment/Supplies _____

Facility Considerations _____

Special Instructions _____

Audience Profile

The audience will be predominantly __ M __ F __ Mixed.

Age group _____

Occupation _____

Education _____

Special Interests _____

Approach

How do I want the audience to perceive me?

What's important to them? What will "speak" to them from *their* perspective?

How will I approach this topic to make it meaningful and memorable for *this* audience?

Model Outline Worksheet

For Topic _____ Page 1 of 2

(Components listed in the order in which they're prepared.)

1. *Objective.* By the end of my presentation, people will:
2. *Key Points.* (The one, two, or three key points that will best support the objective and be meaningful for the audience. What mnemonic device would make them easier to remember?)

    A. _____

      Supporting
      Material

      Transition

    B. _____

      Supporting
      Material

      Transition

    C. _____

      Supporting
      Material

3. Preview.

   Summary.

4. Opener. What will get their attention?

5. Closing "to do". What do I want them to do?

Now, rearrange the components in the order to be presented.

1. Introductory: Opener, objective, and preview
2. Body: Key points, supporting material, transitions
3. Closing: Summary and "to do"

Model Outline Worksheet

For Topic _____ Page 2 of 2

Recognition

What terminology, word choices, and supporting material should I use to correctly address my message to this audience?

Participation

What techniques will I use to involve this audience? to evoke responses from them?

(In parentheses, note point at which the technique is to be inserted: e.g., at the opener, key points, closing)

Rhetorical Questions

Recalls

Scenarios

Application

What statements of value will I relate?

Presentation Review Checklist

For Topic _____ Date _____

Informational   **Observations**

Introductory: __ Opener
               __ Objective
               __ Preview

Body: __ Key Point A
                  __ Supporting material
                  __ Transition
               __ Key Point B
                  __ Supporting material
                  __ Transition
               __ Key Point C
                  __ Supporting material

Closing: __ Summary
               __ "To Do"

Relational

Recognition: __ Addressed to
               __ Affirming
               __ Pacing (variations)

Participation: __ Rhetorical questions
               __ Recalls
               __ Scenarios

Application: __ Value statements

Optimum Delivery

Verbal: __ Clarity
               __ Simplicity
               __ Emotive quality

Vocal: __ Qualities (pitch, volume, rate, tone)
               __ Intonation

Visual: __ Attire and demeanor (presence)
               __ Meaningful eye contact
               __ Platform behavior

Audiovisuals: __ Pictorial   __ Colorful   __ Meaningful

Overall: __ Energetic   __ Enthusiastic   __ Encouraging

Index